STRESS
IN
CHILDREN

STRESS
IN
CHILDREN

How to Recognize, Avoid
and Overcome it

Dr. Bettie B. Youngs

ARBOR HOUSE / New York

Manufactured in the United States of America

10 9 8 7 6 5 4 3 2 1

This book is printed on acid-free paper. The paper in this book meets the guidelines for permanence and durability of the Committee on Production Guidelines for Book Longevity of the Council on Library Resources.

Library of Congress Cataloging in Publication Data

Youngs, Bettie B.
    Stress in children.

    1. Stress in children.   I. Title.
BF723.S75Y68   1985   155.4   85-4013
ISBN 0-87795-684-7 (alk. paper)

To Jennifer Leigh Burres Youngs

CONTENTS

ACKNOWLEDGMENTS

I am grateful to the many people throughout my life who lovingly shared their knowledge with me and contributed to the never-ending process of my learning and understanding. No one's knowledge is ever completely her own, but rather a vast collection of human dynamics and interactions synthesized, intertwined, and then woven into a newly enriched and personalized viewpoint. For me this includes my professional work with thousands of parents, educators, and children, as well as with adults providing services to youngsters throughout the U.S. and abroad.

Specifically, I would like to recognize two exemplary educators. Glen Pinkham and Ardath Bergfall, who in the beginning shaped my desire to become an educator, and Joe D. Batten, who expanded my views and gave me an opportunity to work in nearly thirty countries. A very special thanks to Robert Muller, assistant secretary general in charge of coordinating the work of the thirty-two specialized agencies and world programs of the United Nations, for his friendship and inspiration—and encouragement to write the book "for the evolution of the human family"; and to authors Norman Cousins and Kenneth Pelletier for their wisdom and advice, and for their life-work and teachings, which inspired my desire to teach youngsters the connection between physiological and psychological well-being.

For her counsel, the strength of her commitment to excellence in education, and the warmth of her endearing friendship, Mary Louise Martin; she was invaluable, as was Mary Willia, who kept my own childlike spirit alive and healthy throughout the writing of this book. I must also say thanks to Mary Kennan of Prentice-Hall, who said, "Please go write this book."

Fred Chase of Arbor House was wonderful in his sensitive and supportive editing of this manuscript, and the sustained confidence and support of Bill Thompson at Arbor House was nourishing from start to finish. In addition to being the sort of literary agent writers dream of, Lois de la Haba has been a continuing inspiration to me.

I am grateful to my parents and to Fran and Peter Bilicki for nurturing their son and daughter to be the marvelous people they are, and for colleagues like Rita King, Jack Hill, J. Bruce Francis, Gerald Rosander, Carol Teall, Toni Mannēh, Wendy Rue, and Ray Latta for their support and belief in my work.

The ability of children to be astute social critics never ceases to amaze me. For that I thank the many children who participated in formulating the thesis for this book, and, in particular, my own daughter, Jennifer, who continues to expand my life every day. My special relationship with this darling young girl is undoubtedly central to the views expressed in this book and to my urgent wish to communicate what I have learned.

And, most of all, I wish to acknowledge my husband, for his unconditional love and strength in every facet of my life, and because he was *always* there for me.

Your children are not your children. They are the sons and daughters of life's longing for itself. They come through you but not from you, and though they are with you, yet they belong not to you. You may give them your love, but not your thoughts. For they have their own thoughts. You may house their bodies but not their souls, for their souls dwell in the house of tomorrow, which you cannot visit, not even in your dreams. You may strive to be like them, but seek not to make them like you. For life goes not backward nor tarries with yesterday. You are the bows from which your children as living arrows are sent forth. The archer sees the mark upon the path of the infinite and he bends you to his might that his arrows may go swift and far. Let your bending in the archer's hand be for gladness; for even as he loves the arrow that flies, so he loves also the bow that is stable.

—KAHLIL GIBRAN, *The Prophet*

INTRODUCTION

AS BOTH CHILDREN AND ADULTS, WE ARE TAUGHT
all about health but rarely how to prevent tension. Nor are we
generally taught how to reduce anxiety and stress. Yet the ability
to manage stress is especially necessary in a youngster's life since
so much of his or her existence involves continual change, clarification of values, and forced choices. Unexpected or unfamiliar
situations requiring as-yet-unlearned coping skills produce a
great deal of stress for children. Those children who learn self-
awareness and effective methods for managing the stresses that
occur in everyday life are likely to be healthy and happy and have
a zest and zeal for living. By learning the goals and principles of
coping, children can draw vitality from stress and use it constructively to promote health, fitness, and self-development.

We can better enable our children to have productive and
enjoyable lives during their formative years by helping them to
perceive more adequately their own resources. If youngsters are
to live a more stress-free life, they will need to develop efficient

and effective coping skills in problem-solving, in generating acceptable alternatives to dilemmas, and in dealing with accelerated change. These skills are vital if children are to gain an accurate understanding of the world around them.

How our children will deal with stress as adults is determined to a great extent by what happens during their formative, most impressionable years. Many scientific studies have shown how important early experiences are in influencing later behavior. This is a powerful reason for parents and other concerned adults to make every attempt to help youngsters develop effective stress-managing techniques. In doing so, adults must evaluate their youngsters' capabilities, set reasonable expectations for achievement, and seek to provide youngsters with an opportunity to gain emotional security.

Managing and reducing stress in children requires hard work from parents. Parents must help their children develop their resources, teaching them to focus on their own well-being and uniqueness in order to adjust successfully to the world around them. Stress management emphasizes enhancement of health and well-being through therapeutic and preventive care, physical fitness, and emotional fitness.

Adults must understand the changes their children are experiencing and be aware of their children as social beings. Most of all, we adults need to be able to lessen the negative effects of the extreme pressure and stress our youngsters are experiencing.

There are no easy solutions to reducing stress in children, though it helps to understand the way children develop and the cultural revolution that is transforming so much of American life and spawning new ways of thinking about our children and new expectations about them as well. Youngsters also pay a heavy price for advances in technology and accelerated rates of change, even though the rewards are, or can be, tremendous.

These deep cultural changes (which create a sense of loss for adults as well) give rise to many inconsistencies and contradictions for children. Confronted with a myriad of choices, youngsters grope with each dilemma—and stress is often the result.

The three aspects of life responsible for the most stress:
- abundance of choices
- emphasis on self-fulfillment
- the necessity of satisfying psychological and emotional needs

The concepts and techniques useful in managing stress for both child and adult involve the following:

- awareness
- building networks and support systems
- successful communication
- a healthy self-concept
- cognitive restructuring
- successful problem-solving
- relaxation
- diet
- exercise

These concepts and techniques helpful in coping with stress can be used by children as they act as individuals and by adults as they interact with their children. A series of worksheets designed to enable a child to manage stress effectively is part of the program. It is important that the parents or other significant adults in the child's life study them thoroughly—perhaps to the point of filling in both child and adult sections, imagining when they were children. In this manner they can be prepared to guide children in coping with stress and developing happy and healthy responses to life as they grow to adulthood.

The ways in which we can enrich the lives of the young, help them to gather their resources to cope with the stressors they encounter in their everyday lives—and thus enhance their overall well-being—are what this book is about: *providing information* to better understand what stress is and how it translates into human suffering; *identifying the major sources*—cause and effect—of stress in children; *delineating concepts* to help children learn how they can draw vitality from stress, become more resilient to it, and mobilize their native physiological and psychological defenses; and *teaching children and adults the skills and techniques* to help children effectively manage and reduce their stress.

PART I

THE ORIGINS OF STRESS

ONE

WHAT IS STRESS?

WHEN A YOUNGSTER FALLS FROM A TREE AND IS treated by a doctor for a broken leg, we assume the youngster will recover. Similarly, if a youngster is sick with measles or has an attack of viral flu, we know the child will recover and that with modern medical assistance we can speed up the recovery time and make the youngster as comfortable as possible in the process.

But when a youngster suffers a nervous collapse, an ulcer, repeated psychosomatic illness, lethargy, fatigue, or other health breakdowns, a major cause of the problem is stress—and stress is not so easily or effectively treated.

Stress! A familiar and often-used word these days. Despite our familiarity with the term, it is important to understand exactly what stress is, how it translates into human suffering, how it can be reduced, methods through which we can effectively and productively manage it, and ways in which we can draw vitality from it as well. Equally important is understanding the potential of stress-management techniques in influencing the body's functions and mobilizing our native physiological and psychological defenses.

Stress is the nonspecific response of the body to any demand made upon it. It is a chemical reaction within the body that occurs when there is a basic need to maintain life and to resist or adapt to changing external and internal influences. The body is called upon to adjust in order to maintain normality in response to the stressor. The adrenal glands are the body's prime reactors to stress; the notion that stress is merely terminology or "just in the mind" is simply not true. Stress can be induced by a positive or a negative stimulus. Stress is a reaction of the body to daily events and to our perceptions of these events. To some extent, stress is individualistic: While two individuals may experience the same stressor, their responses may vary. This variety in response gives us the opportunity to influence the body's functions and hence to manage stress as well as draw vitality from it.

Stress has become a major problem in an era characterized by accelerated change and rapid growth of knowledge and technology in an expanding and competitive population. Students in particular pay a high price for stress. Confusion, ambiguity, indifference, rage, and anger result in lost concentration, ineffective use of valuable time, lowered productivity, problems in socialization and friendships, and fewer opportunities to develop individual strengths and capacities.

The "Fight or Flight" Response

As early as the 1920s, Walter Cannon researched organismic responses and identified what has been called the "fight or flight syndrome"—the body's response to the need to protect itself. This syndrome has a predictable pattern and occurs in a wide variety of situations and circumstances. The body is equipped with an instinctive chemical response pattern designed to supply energy in stress situations. The activity of certain glands is triggered by a threat, or stressor, in the body's environment (such as an emotion, a drug, or illness). Each demand made upon the body is unique and specific: When you are too warm, the body perspires in an effort to cool down; when you are too cold, the body shivers to produce more heat.

Similarly, each drug or hormone produces specific actions and responses. The hormone adrenaline, for example, speeds up the pulse rate and blood pressure, simultaneously raising the level of blood sugar. The hormone insulin, conversely, decreases the level of blood sugar. Any imbalance places a demand on the body for readjustment. All stressors to which we are exposed increase the body's need to perform adaptive functions in order to restore itself to a normal state. This adjustment is independent of and in addition to the body's normal activity. *This nonspecific demand for response activity is the essence of stress.*

Our conscious and unconscious efforts to adapt to situations or pressures trigger a chain of biological events. These physiological changes take place in the body processes and the electrochemical system. Stress occurs whenever the body perceives that there is a need either to maintain life or adapt to external and internal imbalancing influences. When the body must adjust to either a positive or negative stressor in order to maintain normal stasis (balance), it undergoes what is called the "general adaptation syndrome." The process through which the human organism responds to stress of any magnitude or duration is called the "stress reaction." The entire body is involved in this process.

A stressful event or chronically stressful condition produces both a physiological and emotional response. Every system of the body is affected at some point in the stress response by nervous stimulation of an organ or of the endocrine glands. The physiological response can best be understood through looking at the following factors:

The hypothalamus, a group of nerves in the brain, makes us aware of events around us. It controls the major regulators of the nervous and immune systems and links the nervous system to the endocrine system. If the hypothalamus is stimulated, it increases the discharge of hormones from this system. The hypothalamus produces substances that activate the pituitary gland at the base of the brain.

When the pituitary gland is activated, adrenocorticotrophic

hormone is sent into the bloodstream. This hormone sets off the secretion of corticoids when it reaches the adrenal glands. Next, the medulla releases adrenaline into the system. This activates the body into a state known as "fight or flight." In this state, heart rate increases, pumping more blood to the vital organs; breathing becomes heavier; eyesight is sharpened; and the mouth becomes "dry." The chemicals released in this process affect the entire body in seconds.

The intensity of the demand for readjustment or adaptation is an important phenomenon to be aware of, since the body's response to intense heat is the same as that to intense cold, intense pain the same as to intense joy. In other words, the stress toll is the same: Each will evoke an identical biochemical reaction in the body.

Thankfully, our body's response to external and internal stressors provides us with signals when we are overloading it. The development of a peptic ulcer in the stomach or intestine is one example of a body's reaction to stress. While an ulcer is a response to the increased level of corticoids in the blood, the autonomic nervous system also plays a role. The glands produce the hormones that stimulate protective bodily responses. In an adaptive response, they gear the body up and attempt to protect it from harm. An ulcer will demand that the individual stop and make an adjustment or adaptation.

A key finding in stress research is that we can facilitate the dissipation of the harmful effects of stress through physical activity. At one time the physical act of fighting or fleeing would have been the typical and highly functional response to stress. But as our society has become more complex and abstract, this is no longer appropriate in most stress situations. Physical assault is not an acceptable response in our society. And because we tend to internalize this stress—holding it in rather than venting it— the excess hormones frequently build up to toxic levels within our bodies.

Stress becomes "distress" when the stress response is too intense or lasts too long. When the delicate internal balance of the physical system malfunctions, it leads eventually to a lowered resistance to illness and to a breakdown of bodily functions—and thus to a stress-related illness. Is it any wonder that stress has been called "the twentieth-century disease"? And that numerous individuals, young and old, suffer from chronic diseases in our stress-filled society?

The Body's Resistance to Stress

After the initial reaction of alarm, the body moves into a period of resistance. This is its attempt to return to its normal balance by adapting to the cause of stress. These physical changes are the same whether the cause of stress is emotional, a disease, or a physical injury. In each case the body attempts to repair the damage, returning itself to a state of balance. If successful, the physical signs of stress disappear: heartbeat and respiration normalize, muscles relax, and resistance to the source of the crisis is released. A serious problem arises when a period of stress is prolonged. If this happens, the adaptation mechanisms are eventually depleted and the body enters the exhaustion stage.

The Exhaustion Response

If the body cannot successfully adapt to the cause of stress, the signs of the alarm reaction appear, even though the damage is now irreversible. In effect, the body has used up all its adaptation energy—it simply isn't able to cope anymore. Sometimes this stage is referred to as "burnout." The supply of life energy and the ability to withstand stress are gone. Tension produces physical wear and tear on the body, and the longer the tension continues, the greater the bodily damage may be.

Youngsters are particularly vulnerable to stress. They often lead multidimensional lives with fast-paced life-styles. They spend great portions of energy quickly and become prime targets for fatigue, moodiness, psychosomatic illness, migraines, ulcers, asthma, ulcerative colitis, endocrine-gland disorders, and other diseases of adaptation, including burnout. Although everyone, including children, must tolerate a certain degree of discomfort from stress in modern living, it is clear that chronic stress prolonged beyond reasonable bounds can precipitate major health breakdowns.

While recognizing the usefulness of some degree of stress in our lives, most medical researchers now believe that the chemical effects of stress within the human body are causative factors in most contemporary health breakdowns. As will be seen later in the book, medical researchers also believe them to be linked to many other medical and physical disorders.

Individual Response to Stress

While stress is no more than anxiety or physical nervousness to some individuals, in others it can lead to emotional despair, psychosomatic illness, and even mental illness. When an individual is forced to adapt or to readjust to an event, the reaction occurs in both the mind and the body. Why some individuals become ill and others do not under the same stressful conditions is determined to a great extent by the individual's interpretation of the stressor.

TWO

THE PSYCHOLOGICAL RESPONSE TO STRESS

IN DISCUSSING THE PSYCHOLOGICAL RESPONSE TO stress, we must first look at its effects in psychosomatic terms. The word *psychosomatic* refers to bodily and mental symptoms stemming from mental conflict. The basis of the psychosomatic concept is that the mind plays an important role in many diseases. Psychosomatic illnesses fall into two basic categories: psychogenic and somatogenic.

Psychogenic Disorders

Psychogenic disorders are physical diseases caused by emotional stress. Actual structural and functional organ damage occurs in such cases, yet none of the usual underlying physical causes of organic disease is present. Bronchial asthma, peptic ulcers, high blood pressure, migraine headaches, and backaches are examples of conditions that may fall into this category. Specific disorders are usually brought about when an individual is not coping effectively within his or her surroundings. Such emotional turmoil is translated into physical symptoms.

Somatogenic Disorders

The somatogenic phenomenon has far-reaching implications for health and the mind-body relationship. Emotional disturbances increase the body's susceptibility to organic diseases and infections. When an individual is under more stress than he is able to handle, latent infection can be converted by stressful disturbances into organic disease. A healthy body fights off many invading organisms through its natural defense mechanisms, but distress impedes the body's natural defensive role and the result is a breakdown of physical health. Intense or prolonged stress may accelerate the rate at which disease spreads throughout the body by hampering the body's natural immune system. Indeed, the onset or dissipation of severe stress in an individual's life may be the deciding factor in bringing on or warding off disease.

Thought alone can increase or decrease our internal arousal. It holds the key to understanding emotional well-being and provides opportunities for stress management by making it possible to maintain a high level of psychological and physiological stability.

The Relationship of Attitudes to Stress and Disease

Research is still being undertaken on the ways in which emotional well-being contributes to physical well-being: what role a specific set of attitudes may have in determining an individual's overall "wellness." The research is surprising and challenging.

We know, for example, that there are professions in which individuals develop stress-related symptoms and even diseases that often lead to death during certain rush seasons or in traumatic career setbacks or change. We also know that the death of a spouse or child and separation or divorce increase one's chances of becoming ill. In addition, some individuals who have seemingly easier occupations develop ulcers, colitis, migraine headaches, hypertension, heart disease, cancer, and other stress-related symptoms. Still other individuals find it impossible to cope with the problems of everyday life without becoming emotionally and physically ill.

Similarly, and contrary to these examples, we can cite the reverse: individuals who hold demanding and exhausting jobs and who thrive on what they consider the excitement of being involved in high-pressure environments.

Studies do not indicate that such individuals become "stress-resistant." What the studies reveal is that such people are motivated by challenge and commitment and have a feeling of involvement in whatever they are doing and a sense of control over their lives. We know now that these attitudes have a profound effect on health—on the individual's overall emotional and physical well-being. These individuals perceive themselves as interacting in a positive manner with their environment. They develop a specific set of positive attitudes that facilitate flexibility, and they exhibit a sound process in generating viable alternatives to problems and obstacles at an early age. They are likely to display popular posters that read, "Life is a journey to be lived, not a problem to be solved," or "When you get lemons, make lemonade."

This supports the contention that stress resides neither in the person alone nor in the situation alone, but depends on how the person appraises the situation and that while the mechanism whereby stressful events produce illness is presumably physiological, personality "hardiness" may decrease the likelihood of breakdown into illness.

The results of many studies reveal that high-stress/low-illness individuals stand out in three main categories: (1) they are much more actively involved in their work and social lives than those who become ill under stress; (2) they tend to accept and even embrace challenge; and (3) they feel more in control of events in their lives.

Now researchers are attempting to determine whether major changes in an individual's life necessarily result in debilitating stress. The Holmes-Rahe Stress Scale, for example, measures and gives specific weight to all the recent changes in a person's life in forty-two areas of change and assumes that any major change is stressful. The scale begins with a 100-point score for the death of a spouse and descends to such changes as vacations (13). Participants are asked to note the changes that occurred in their lives in the last twelve months and calculate their scores. According to the scale, the more change a person experiences, the more likely that person is to get sick.

We are beginning to realize, however, that some changes in an individual's routine can be beneficial and even necessary for stimulation and growth. It is also felt that the effects of stress depend largely on the ability to cope with stressors. Those who thrive on challenge are much more likely to transform events to their advantage and thus reduce the intensity of stressors. Those individuals who have strong commitment also take an active role in their work and family lives. They tend to view their activities as interesting, important, and as having an impact on their surroundings. These attitudes give them a feeling of being in control of their lives and their surroundings, another element of psychological hardiness.

In contrast, people who rate low in psychological hardiness may use avoidance techniques in coping. Excessive use or abuse of alcohol and drugs, using tranquilizers, excessive TV viewing are all self-defeating tactics since they only alleviate stress for a short while. Stress continues to exert its debilitating effects on these people since it remains in the mind unassimilated and unaltered—an issue of endless rumination and subconscious preoccupation.

The fact that there is room for personal response in managing stress gives us an opportunity to help individuals confront and deal with it. We know that specific aspects of personality interact with specific aspects of the social environment in many ways, leading to greater or less resilience, and that such factors as physiological predisposition, early childhood experiences, and personality and social resources affect an individual's reaction to stress. For this reason, we need to know more about the expectations and social pressures that our youngsters feel in our concern about their psychological well-being.

Social supports such as family, friends, colleagues, and significant others are vital in protecting people from illness. Adults with a strong sense of social ties—marriage, friends, family, relatives, support groups, etc.—have far lower mortality rates than those without such ties.

For youngsters, a good picture of social support is provided by a study of children in a kibbutz. The social support provided by life in a kibbutz seems to protect children against even the anxiety one would expect as a result of prolonged military bombardment. In 1975, a time of heavy Arab shelling in certain parts of the country, an Israeli researcher compared the anxiety levels of children in several kibbutz and urban communities, in both bombed and tranquil areas. Although urban children who had lived through prolonged bombardment had higher anxiety levels than those from tranquil urban areas, the kibbutz children did not show any difference: Their anxiety levels were low regardless of whether their kibbutz had been shelled. During bombardments, kibbutz children were calmly led to shelters that were familiar to them and where education programs and social life went on pretty much as usual. On the other hand, the urban children, accustomed to living in family units, were suddenly taken to alien and somewhat disordered community shelters. Their higher anxiety level could be explained by the disruption of their normal daily routine and social network.

The Mind and Illness

Many experts believe that many diseases are nothing other than the expression of a person's need to withdraw for a while from the frays and strains of living, and that even death is sometimes an individual's way of ending a painful emotional struggle, of resolving an emotional conflict. Many are also convinced that psychological forces play an important role in the development of cancer and that psychological forces can be mobilized to defeat or delay its course.

The belief that mind and body affect each other, in sickness and in health, has gained a good deal of respectability over the past couple of decades. The rise of the holistic health movement has given added impetus to the view that the mental and the physical are different aspects of the very same entity—the integrated, whole human being. Clearly, a healthy body is the result of a healthy mind.

THREE

CHANGE AS A STRESSOR

VAST AND SWEEPING CHANGES HAVE OCCURRED IN this century—dramatic shifts in our life-styles, attitudes, habits, thoughts, beliefs, organizational structures, health patterns, and methods of coping. Along with this, equally significant changes have been made in terms of what society expects from youngsters. As social dis-ease increases, it is manifested directly in the schools and in the children.

Because we were born into this Age of Stress, many of us may not be aware of the incredible changes that have been occurring in this century. Karl Albrecht has traced five major changes that have contributed greatly to stress and burnout among all industrialized nations and their people.

From Rural to Urban Living

First and foremost, we have moved from rural to urban living. In 1900, 40 percent of Americans lived in urban areas. By 1975 the number had increased to 75 percent. And in urban areas, the crowding and pace contribute to increased anxiety. Our culture has also changed from a stationary to a mobile one. Time is of the essence—being on time, doing things quickly, getting places fast. Our cultural change from self-sufficiency to "throwaway" consumerism has added to our stress by depriving us of a feeling of permanence and stability. We have also moved from isolation to interconnectedness—primarily as a result of the "global village" TV has spawned—and this further increases our stress as we become intimate with all the horrors of the globe on TV every night. And finally, we are now a sedentary rather than active society, decreasing our body's strength and increasing its susceptibility to stress.

Change as a Stressor

Because of vast technological advances and accelerated rates of change, we have been able to view within a shorter span of time—and at closer range—profound and new qualities in our children. Many adults—and youngsters as well—speak ambiguously about these qualities. They are generally confused about societal changes, sometimes feel alienated and isolated because of the accelerated rate of those changes, and baffled by the myriad decisions and choices with which children must contend.

Culture has a dynamic thrust of its own. In place of once traditional ethics of self-denial and sacrifice, we now find an ethic under which people refuse to deny themselves anything. They place a high priority on personal life and the quality of that life. This new search for self-fulfillment is a powerful force, causing people to want more control over life and the ability to transform their lives if they please. The new, the unfamiliar create personal struggles that are often painful and certainly bewildering. It appears as though we are making a decisive break with shared meanings of the past.

But one fact remains constant: In nurturing our young, we adults need to understand those dimensions of change and their relationship to youngsters as social beings. Most of all, we need to be able to lessen the negative effects of the extreme pressure and stress that our youngsters are experiencing.

I mentioned in the introduction that there are three issues responsible for the most stress in children:

- abundance of choices
- emphasis on self-fulfillment
- the necessity of satisfying physiological and psychological needs

Here is how they work.

A. **Dilemma**

An *abundance of choices* about what to do with one's life but insufficient knowledge of how to make the right choice.

Stress

Because of the high value of personal freedom, each new choice and commitment is considered a threat to that freedom and a challenge to the other options that might also be exercised. The question of what commitment and sacrifice to make is unsettling.

B. **Dilemma**

The *chance for self-fulfillment* and success presupposes a cooperative economic and social environment. Personal goals depend on an affluent economy, a host of career opportunities, flexible work arrangements, low-cost travel, diverse outlets for personal creativity, and few burdens of responsibility.

Stress

Today's low-growth, inflationary economic environment, with its troubling undercurrent of sociopolitical stress, fosters less hospitable conditions for many self-fulfillment goals.

C. **Dilemma**

The *preoccupation with physiological and psychological*

needs places a continual emphasis on the desires of the self. Emotions are sacred, and unfulfilled needs are profane.

Stress

This psychological attitude affects precisely those crisis points in one's life when attention might more productively be turned outward toward the world and its vicissitudes.

Among the many new realities with which youngsters must contend:

- New fields of work
- Creativity as a life-style
- Changing definitions of success
- Viable options in self-fulfillment
- More-convenient norms of domestic life
- A free conscience—perceptions of being free to choose
- Emphasis on making fewer sacrifices
- Expectation of enjoying the warmth of relationships and/ or family along with the freedom to choose
- Defining new rules; redefining old ones
- Expectation of psychological satisfaction from a job
- Desire for personal autonomy
- Expectation of being treated with "dignity," "fairness," and "justice"
- Introspective thinking/problem-solving
- New social ethic of commitment
- Emphasis on closer, deeper personal relationships
- Emphasis on placing professional and private lives on a more equal footing

Need, growth, self-actualization, potential. These words are now frequently used in a youngster's psychological vocabulary. Children assume that the words characterize a private, autonomous, culture-free self. These assumptions are so deeply rooted that it is difficult, if not impossible, to fully extricate them. In part, this view causes stress to both the individual and society since the individual is not actually fulfilled in becoming more autonomous. In fact, to move too far in this direction is to risk alienation and loneliness.

Many youngsters still maintain traditional values, though they question some of the behavior patterns that such values presume. For example, in the past, self-achievement meant worldly success; today, it more likely means thoughtful improvement of the self. Not all of the cultural changes are new; rather, the cultural meaning of the changes has a new emphasis. Changes in the female work population, for example, reflect a marked shift in social meanings. A shared meaning equating masculinity with earning power persisted until the late 1960s. Now the two-paycheck family is rapidly becoming the norm, accounting for a majority of upper-income households. This adjustment requires new definitions based on new shared meanings.

It is futile to consider these changes as setbacks, or merely as a time to get through, for they are here whether we like them or not. If we view them positively, we can improve the quality of life and not merely adjust to the loss of traditional mores. Indeed, we may find that a new range of positive life choices will result in greater fulfillment and a new ethic of commitment that will strike a better balance in our lives. This fulfillment and commitment could turn out to be bonuses for our children.

The process of developing new social signals, transmitting them, and assimilating them will no doubt take some time, but will be worth the time and commitment involved. We are faced with an extraordinary challenge: How do we preserve warmth and closeness and at the same time hold on to the new freedom to choose? According to Daniel Yankelovich, that is the preeminent question about our domestic lives that is now confronting our culture.

The sweeping changes in marriage, family life, and the relationship to children fill many people with sadness and nostalgia. The changes create a sense of loss, almost of grief, and give rise to many inconsistencies and contradictions. A large number of people who express a reduced commitment of parents to children and children to parents also wish to see a return to more traditional standards of family life and parental responsibility.

Why the contradiction? People may claim that they want to return to the family life of the past, but when it comes to the specifics of day-to-day living, very few—male or female—have any hankering to return to traditional standards of sexual relations, to the spic-and-span housekeeping norms of the past, or to the male monopoly on working outside the home. Americans long for the warmth and closeness they associate with family life in earlier decades, but not at the cost of going back to the old repressive rules.

PART II

CAUSES
OF STRESS
IN CHILDREN

FOUR

THE DECLINE IN
"CHILDHOOD"

THERE ARE, OF COURSE, NUMEROUS REASONS WHY
our culture is providing fewer opportunities for children to experience childhood. The modern effects of technology, media
ecology, and changing social and individual values are quickly
altering our psychological and social perceptions of children.

Childhood as we know it today signifies a distinct state of life.
In other words, this period of years is set apart as a time when
the young are "trained"; they learn how to be adults—hopefully,
utilizing their uniqueness as they do so. This has not always been
so, for the idea of childhood is not very old.

Prior to the sixteenth century, the idea of childhood hardly
existed in the Western world. This was particularly true for youngsters once they were six or seven years of age. The language of
children, their dress, their games, their labor, and their legal
rights were the same as those of adults. There were no special
institutions for the nurturing of children, nor were there books
on child rearing or parenthood. Because mortality rates were

extraordinarily high, children were not mentioned in wills and testaments—an indication that adults did not expect them to live to adulthood. Rarely were portraits made of children, but if there were, they usually depicted them as small adults, devoid of any of the physical characteristics of childhood. They were not regarded as fundamentally different from adults. In other words, by seven years of age, childhood was already over.

Expanding Childhood

Less than 100 years after Gutenberg's invention of the printing press, the European culture became a reading culture. As a result, childhood was redefined, beginning in the fifteenth century. One could not become an adult unless one knew how to read, and since reading skills are best learned while oral language is being acquired, the young were separated and sent to a place established for the purpose—that is, a school. For the first time, the young were set apart and recognized as a special class of people whose minds and character were qualitatively different from those of adults. Segregating this group also helped us recognize human development as a series of stages, with childhood as a bridge between infancy and adulthood.

Shortening Childhood

We are now witnessing yet another transformation—the erasing of the dividing line between childhood and adulthood. Childhood innocence and specialness are now almost impossible to sustain. Many facets of life once regarded as being for adults only—such as life's mysteries, its contradictions, its violence, its tragedies, and sexual, physical, and social responsibilities—are no longer off limits to children. In part the new age of television erases the dividing line between childhood and adulthood since it does not segregate its audience; it communicates the same information to everyone simultaneously, regardless of sex, age, race, or level of education. All varieties of life are broadcast for everyone, including children, to view: homosexuality, divorce, corruption, sadism, adult madness, promiscuity, incest, and other sensationalist topics.

Is the concept of childhood at an end? Like the paintings of earlier centuries, children on television and in everyday life are once again depicted as small adults. The language, dress, sexuality, and even interests of children are not so different from those of adults. They are not shielded from adult secrets or from the behavior of adults engaged in discussing or acting out those secrets.

But if our traditional concept of childhood is becoming less relevant to the current situation, it is not because we are immersed in an adult world *per se*. Our world, rather, is more a projection of the adult child—a new kind of person with an obsessive need for immediate gratification, a lack of concern for consequences, and an almost promiscuous preoccupation with consumption.

Present-Day Transformation

This new transformation makes the behaviors, attitudes, desires, and even physical appearance of adults and children indistinguishable: Children are now committing crimes once attributed to adults only; clothing styles for children copy those designed for adults; games meant only for children are rapidly disappearing; children's games are becoming "sports," supervised with adult rules and regulations; children commonly use language once reserved for adults and not even to be uttered in the presence of children; children are rarely shielded from information regarding adult secrets; food, music, literature are shared; legal rights of children are similar to those of adults.

Why Is Childhood Disappearing?

There are a myriad of answers to this question: availability and accessibility of the electronic media; disruption of the nuclear family and loss of importance of the extended family; increased mobility and home-shifting; elimination of old forms of labor and the introduction of the possibility of career alternatives; and the declining birthrate—to scratch the surface.

Why should we be concerned with fewer opportunities for children to experience childhood? As adults, we need to be children first, or we will never develop feelings of belonging, the capacity for lasting relationships, respect for limits. Being a child is just plain natural and an essential part of life.

FIVE

THE HURRIED CHILD

THE AMERICAN CHILD HAS BECOME THE UNWILL-ing, unintended victim of overwhelming stress born of rapid, bewildering social change and constantly rising expectations. Children these days are under extraordinary pressure to achieve, to succeed, to please. They are constantly being hurried. By hurrying our children to grow up, by treating them as adults, we are lightening our burdens at their expense. We are enlisting their aid in carrying life's baggage.

The "hurried child"—David Elkind's term—is often forced to assume the physical, psychological, and social trappings of adulthood before he or she is prepared to do so. We dress our children in miniature adult costumes, expose them to gratuitous sex and violence, and expect them to cope with an increasingly changing social environment of divorce, single parenthood, and other problems that did not exist for previous generations. Hurried children seem to comprise a large portion of the troubled young patients seeking psychiatric help, of students failing in school, of students involved in delinquency and drugs, of suicides. Hurried children are among those who have chronic psychosomatic complaints such as headaches and stomachaches, who are chronically unhappy, who are hyperactive, lethargic, or unmotivated.

Do you hurry your children? Are you guilty of rushing your child through childhood? David Elkind's "Hurry Sickness" Quiz will help you determine if you are in fact pushing your child too hard to accomplish unreachable goals.

"HURRY SICKNESS" QUIZ

Please indicate how often each of the following applies to you in daily life.

1. Do you find yourself rushing your speech? 1 2 3 4 5
2. Do you hurry other people's speech by interrupting them with "umhm, umhm" or by completing their sentences for them? 1 2 3 4 5
3. Do you hate to wait in line? 1 2 3 4 5
4. Do you seem to be short of time to get everything done? 1 2 3 4 5
5. Do you detest wasting time? 1 2 3 4 5
6. Do you eat too fast? 1 2 3 4 5
7. Do you drive over the speed limit? 1 2 3 4 5
8. Do you try to do more than one thing at a time? 1 2 3 4 5
9. Do you become impatient if others do something too slowly? 1 2 3 4 5
10. Do you seem to have little time to relax and enjoy the time of day? 1 2 3 4 5
11. Do you find yourself overcommitted? ... 1 2 3 4 5
12. Do you jiggle your knees or tap your fingers? 1 2 3 4 5
13. Do you think about other things during conversations? 1 2 3 4 5
14. Do you walk fast? 1 2 3 4 5
15. Do you hate dawdling after a meal? 1 2 3 4 5

16. Do you become irritable after a meal? .. 1 2 3 4 5
17. Do you detest losing in sports or games? 1 2 3 4 5
18. Do you find yourself with clenched fists
    or tight neck or jaw muscles? 1 2 3 4 5
19. Does your concentration sometimes wan-
    der while you think about what's coming
    up later?................................. 1 2 3 4 5
20. Are you a competitive person?........... 1 2 3 4 5

RULE-OF-THUMB INTERPRETATION

20–60   OK
61–79   Needs Improvement
80 +   Time Bomb!

Never

Rarely

Sometimes

Often

Always

One of the most significant and disturbing trends of recent years is the troubled generation of teenagers who, according to a *U.S. News & World Report* study, are "unable to cope with the pressures of growing up in what they perceive as a world that is hostile and indifferent to them." Teenagers today are subjected to stress far greater than that experienced by earlier generations. Statistics that measure social behavior bear witness to these sad truths:

• One-third of the major crimes in America are committed by people under twenty years of age.

- Fifteen percent of high-school students are considered problem drinkers. Alcohol is the leading youth-behavior-modification problem.
- Nearly one-third of all violent-crime arrests are of teen-agers.
- One out of every ten teenagers between thirteen and seventeen years of age become pregnant (one million).
- Among fifteen-to-twenty-year-olds, suicide is the third leading cause of death after homicide and accidents. There are about 2,000 teenage suicides a year.
- One-third of all American school-age children use illegal drugs.

Children are often a good barometer of what is taking place in the home. When family problems or stress occur, children may act out or demonstrate through their behavior the way they are feeling about those events or interactions. A young child whose parents are going through a divorce, for example, may indirectly express anxiety by manifesting physical symptoms of that stress through headaches or stomachaches.

Sometimes we fail to detect family stress because we focus on the behavior of the youngster and do not attempt to discover the cause of the behavior. We speak about youngsters going through a "rebellious stage," often without identifying the cause.

If we are to detect family stress, we must develop an awareness of the types of situations and events that are common to all families and that often induce stress for those involved.

There are two major sources of family stress. The first category is comprised of events external to family members: life-threatening events (illness; death of a family member, close relative or significant other; divorce; move to a new city; change in jobs, parental careers). Also included in this category are natural changes in the life cycle of each member, children and adults. Changes caused by the various developmental stages of childhood, adolescence, young adulthood, etc., create new behavioral and emotional changes that have an impact not only on the individual undergoing change but on other family members as well.

The second major source of family stress is psychological and emotional difficulties experienced by a family member. These changes, too, affect the entire family system. Children in particular often experience anger and resentment—and sometimes guilt about being angry—at the person who has problems, because the problems have upset family equilibrium.

Detecting Family Stress

One way to detect family stress is to examine the behavioral/emotional manifestations of the stressors. Children will act out, misbehave, exhibit lost concentration, do poorly in school, and may develop psychosomatic problems. It becomes necessary to trace back to when and where the problems began. It is important to ask a series of questions that explore the changes and events that have occurred within the family. Asking the right questions and finding appropriate answers can prevent emotional overreacting and/or miscommunication between family members. Once the causes have been detected, open communication, a primary requirement for preventing unnecessary family stress, can begin. Another important facet is *active listening*—a technique that will help youngsters clarify their feelings. By active listening, you restate what the other person has said so that he or she can know that the listener understands, and so both can understand the problem more clearly.

An open exchange of feelings and mutual problem-solving can be a tremendously valuable vehicle for managing stress within the family. The Coping Scale will help you assess how effectively you are coping now. Later I will discuss specific ways to improve stress-coping of both parents and children. Only when parents learn effective ways to cope can they influence the behavior of their youngsters.

COPING SCALE

A number of ways people react to stress and tension are given below. Please indicate your own rating on each item by circling one of the five numbers at the right of each item. Please do not skip any items. There are no right or wrong answers.

WHEN I AM FEELING STRESS AND TENSION...

1. I use alcoholic beverages. 1   2   3   4   5
2. I talk it out with others. 1   2   3   4   5
3. I try to find out more about the
   situation..................................... 1   2   3   4   5
4. I daydream................................. 1   2   3   4   5
5. I rely on my belief in a supernatural power
   who cares about me........................ 1   2   3   4   5
6. I work it off by physical exercise......... 1   2   3   4   5
7. I try to see the humorous aspects of the
   situation..................................... 1   2   3   4   5
8. I don't worry about it; everything will
   probably work out fine..................... 1   2   3   4   5
9. I sleep more. 1   2   3   4   5
10. I take some definite action on the basis
    of my present understanding. 1   2   3   4   5
11. I draw on my past experience............ 1   2   3   4   5
12. I use food and food substitutes (smoking,
    chewing gum, eating more). 1   2   3   4   5
13. I prepare myself for the worst. 1   2   3   4   5
14. I curse...................................... 1   2   3   4   5
15. I make several alternate plans for han-
    dling the situation......................... 1   2   3   4   5
16. I use drugs. 1   2   3   4   5
17. I become involved in other activities to
    keep my mind off the problem........... 1   2   3   4   5
18. I cry.. 1   2   3   4   5

Never

Seldom

Sometimes

Usually

Always

INTERPRETATION

In general, the more long-term coping mechanisms you employ, the better, although sometimes a short-term mechanism is very useful and occasionally a long-term one is not useful. The mechanisms listed above are classified as follows:

1. Short-term	10. Long-term
2. Long-term	11. Long-term
3. Long-term	12. Short-term
4. Short-term	13. Short-term
5. Long-term	14. Short-term
6. Long-term	15. Long-term
7. Short-term	16. Short-term
8. Short-term	17. Short-term
9. Short-term	18. Short-term

(Reproduced courtesy of Janice Bell. Adapted from J. M. Bell, "Stressful Life Events and Coping Methods in Mental-illness and -wellness Behaviors." *Nursing Research* 26(2), 1977: 136-41.)

Many youngsters, beset by the pressure to grow up quickly, become jaded by their mid-teens and are unable to cope with the kinds of problems facing them. Among thousands of teenagers, alienation and a lack of clear moral standards now prevail to the point where individuals, families, and in some instances whole communities are threatened.

This is not to imply that the vast majority of young Americans emerge from their teens in a helpless state. On the contrary— the youth of today are generally responsible, caring, concerned, questing. Nevertheless, the percentage of troubled children is rising dramatically. Many youngsters suffer stress and depression from being bounced from one divorced parent to another. Children from middle- and upper-income families are under constant pressure to excel in sports or academics, to be popular, to enroll in good colleges and pursue lucrative professional careers. Those in the inner cities remain largely unemployed and are trapped in their despair. "Burnouts" languish on street corners, in video-game arcades, in school parking lots or foster-care centers. One side effect of this meager existence is what are known as socio-pathic subcultures, ranging from membership in religious cults and extremist groups to the demented punk-rock underground.

Psychologist David Elkind, chairman of the Tufts University School of Child Development and author of *The Hurried Child*, says, "Many young people lost their moorings in the turmoil over Vietnam, Watergate, racial unrest, drug abuse and violence. The 'me first' or 'do your own thing' philosophy is the way these people are raising their children." The upshot is that loneliness, boredom, and rebelliousness are prevalent among youngsters and that disaffection with life runs deep in youth in every level of society.

Clearly, we must value childhood. It is a vital period in life to which children are entitled. It is a child's *right* to be a child. In fact, childhood is the most basic right of children.

SIX

THE HOME ENVIRONMENT

WE ALL WANT OUR CHILDREN TO LEAD PRODUCT-
ive, happy lives. Few parents would disagree with that as a common goal. Yet in coping with the everyday demands of work,
unforeseen dilemmas, persistent pressures and responsibilities of
parenting, parents can, and often do, inflict undue suffering upon
their children, who bear the brunt of such mounting parental
frustrations. In coping with complex agendas and complex problems (such as divorce), given the performance expectation of our
multifaceted roles, is it any wonder that our youngsters are scapegoats to our anxieties?

How can we best keep our children from becoming scapegoats?
How can we best enrich their lives and provide the psychological
comforts so vital to the formative years of those lives? We are in
need of creative and innovative ways to minimize their trauma.

Causes and Effects

We are increasingly aware of the effects stress has upon our youngsters—of the physiological, psychological, and academic rami-

fications. They are largely summed up in the accompanying
table, "Manifestations of Stress in Three Areas."

MANIFESTATIONS OF STRESS
IN THREE AREAS

HUMAN	SOCIAL	SCHOOL ENVIRONMENT
Alcohol abuse		
Anorexia	Accidents	Absenteeism
Anxiety	Adjustment	Diminished memory
Apathy	problems	Disruption
Boredom	Alienation	Increased errors
Burnout	Cynicism	Indecisiveness
Depression	Defensive	Lack of commitment
Diet abuse	behavior	Lack of
Drug abuse	Detachment	concentration
Emotional	Dissatisfaction	Reduced productivity
instability	Distrust	Thefts
Fatigue	Excessive use of	Unpreparedness
Frustration	escape	
Health	Irresponsibility	
breakdowns	Irritability	
Helplessness	Mechanisms	
Hopelessness	Physical abuse	
Insecurity	Resentment	
Lack of self-	Role conflicts	
control	Thefts	
Lack of self-	Vandalism	
respect	Verbal abuse	
Self-neglect	Violence	
Suicide		
Vitamin abuse		

These conditions work against our efforts and reduce chances
for meaningful and nourishing experiences to enhance the psychological and physical well-being of youngsters. We must pro-

vide opportunities that guide, motivate, and encourage children by increasing their ability to handle themselves more effectively within various environments, with peers and the adult world. The goal is to help youngsters

- see the world from another, more positive viewpoint
- become aware of how they personally contribute to and enhance their own lives
- learn skills for understanding themselves
- improve their ability to relate to others
- develop confidence
- gain proficiency in managing stress

In minimizing the stressors that occur in youngsters' lives, we must function effectively as adults. We must seek solutions to our problems, resolve our conflicts, care for others, and look for satisfaction in our own lives.

What can we do to become effective, caring, and competent? How can we learn to be good to ourselves and to others? What measures can we take in order to stop using our youngsters as scapegoats, to help them live a "whole" life and successfully negotiate the living experience? The following skills and suggestions—focused on both parents and youngsters—have proven helpful.

FOR PARENTS

Recognize good behavior as well as bad. Praise achievement and good citizenship. Remember that a youngster's self-esteem is crucial to satisfactory behavior.

Talk with your children. Set aside times for talking, preferably when emotions are not high. Encourage your children to express their opinions and feelings. Encourage questions and answer them fully.

Have fun with your children. Have regular family projects and games. Read together, share what you read, and discuss points of view. When parents and children interact and have fun together, harmony is created and fewer problems requiring discipline arise.

Watch for signs of problems and seek professional help whenever it seems needed. Be on the alert for poor schoolwork, truancy, absenteeism, and poor citizenship marks on report cards. If you see your child slipping into negative behaviors that you cannot correct by yourself, consider help from school counselors, teachers, school principals, psychologists, clergy or community service agencies. (School counselors in most districts' guidance-services department can help you contact community agencies that serve young people and their families.)

Set high expectations for courtesy, citizenship, and responsibility. Establish goals for your children that relate to specific standards you yourself adhere to.

Decide on reasonable, clear rules and enforce them consistently. Make only those rules that you believe to be truly important, to which the child can adhere, and that you intend to enforce. If your child breaks a rule, the consequences should be certain, prompt, and related directly to the offense. And remember, punishment has impact because of its certainty, not because of its severity.

Encourage your children to respect authority and explain why it is important for them to do so. Explain the need for rules and the need for such rules to be obeyed.

Be involved in what goes on in your child's life. Attend his/her functions. Talk with teachers, counselors, and school administrators as often as possible. Be aware of what goes on in your child's life.

Shelter youngsters from undue concerns. Generally, youngsters should remain somewhat sheltered from family financial worries, job uncertainties, and other economic realities, since forcing children to face threats to their basic security produces only anxiety. Adults are powerful symbols of authority for youngsters. They set limits, mediate and interpret the world. Here are some suggestions.

• *A predictable environment* reduces stress that comes

from confronting the unknown. Thus adults should provide a relatively stable environment and encourage youngsters to follow a predictable schedule. Visual display of this schedule reinforces for the child its familiar pattern. While adults often tire of routine, youngsters enjoy it.

- *Youngsters need a measure of their progress.* Adults can help by graphically illustrating children's individual progress, by comparing the extent of the knowledge youngsters have already mastered with the extent of the knowledge they still must acquire, or by comparing the current state of a youngster's knowledge with the state of his knowledge at some previous point. If the child knows his status and understands the expectations of significant adults, the stress that ambiguity often brings can be reduced.

- *Adults must help youngsters set levels of expectation* that challenge but do not overwhelm.

- *Children need practice in meeting demands similar to those they will face as adults.* Therefore, adults should occasionally provide youngsters with experiences that engender mild frustration. Tolerance for stress is best built gradually. Although it might not always come easily, success should always be a possibility, never completely beyond the grasp of the child.

- *Help youngsters develop inner controls.* Rules are an important first step. Posted reminders provide visual reinforcements.

- *Help youngsters learn responsible behavior.* Reinforce the concept that behavior always carries consequences. This reduces the ambiguity of rules and expectations, and simultaneously helps children to willingly adjust their behavior to meet social expectations.

- *Adults should develop reasonable, clearly stated disciplinary policies.* Punishment, if used, should be applied fairly, immediately, in proportion to the offense, and without recrimination. Children should always see the possibility and the necessity of making a fresh start.

- *Adults should encourage youngsters to talk about their fears* and should be willing to supply facts—appropriate to the age group—that rationally explain those human behaviors and events that might otherwise touch off youngsters' irrational fears.
- *Adults must provide comfort, support, and understanding* to children who face stressful situations such as parental divorce, a death in the family, an accident, an illness or other major crises that strain the coping abilities of children and make them more reliant on adult support.

Nurture a zestful approach to living. Teaching youngsters a healthy and zestful life experience requires an approach to living that maximizes rational self-fulfillment and minimizes stress and burnout. This includes fostering and teaching youngsters enjoyment of the love and support of family and friends, enjoyment of constructive and productive work, and added self-fulfillment through meeting new and exciting growth challenges. The following activities bring youngsters closer to success in those endeavors:

- *Mind-stretching activities* primarily involve self-study and individualized learning activities to broaden one's personal horizons and to experience the warm glow of personal growth and achievement. Mind-stretching activities place heavy emphasis on imagination and personal creativity; the possibilities are as limitless as the range of the unfamiliar to a given person. Remember, the body may be confined, but the mind is always free to roam and explore.
- *Arts and crafts* offer socialization, year-round pursuit, and self-training and require only a minimal financial outlay to launch on an exploratory basis. Arts and crafts offer many educational, creative, and relaxation benefits.
- *Avocational activities with moneymaking potential*

overlap arts and crafts, but extend beyond them with the potential of marketing one's work.

- *Collecting things* is fun, opens new worlds to a learner, provides opportunities for socialization and sharing, and often offers financial gain.
- *Growing things* can result in beautification of one's environment, provide for sharing with others, offer healthy outdoor activity and a good learning experience, and contribute to a more nutritious diet.
- *Nature and outdoor activities* promote mental, physical, and spiritual wholeness in addition to providing many opportunities for creativity and learning.
- *Social service* caters to a person's basic need for moral, spiritual and ethical expression and development. "Adopting" others within a helping context is one of the best ways to get on the outside of our own problems and stresses.
- *Sports, games, and related activities* satisfy the need for wholesome physical and mental activity in addition to holding promise for a longer life-span through promotion of sound physical health. The social aspect of such activities is also important. A range of activities is possible, from active participation to spectatorship.
- *Travel*, although constantly growing more expensive, is financially accessible in some form to everyone. Travel offers well-rounded educational experience as well as mental and physical relaxation.

Help youngsters develop a healthy adjustment to the realities of life. We must first understand that adult perceptions of reality often differ from those of youngsters. Stress is an invisible part of life, and while our goal is to shield youngsters from undue stress, we must help them develop healthy adjustments to the realities of life. Our goal must be to help them develop healthy responses and a sense of competence rather than recurring frustration that generates permanent feelings of inadequacy and insecurity. Youngsters generally perceive adults as those in charge.

They bring order out of chaos, correct wrongs, balance injustices, and control the forces that would otherwise prove overwhelming. Generally, youngsters see adults in authority as protective and benign.

Youngsters need defined limits in order to develop self-control. Physical and psychological limits make the world more manageable, more secure, more understandable. Limits create a more predictable environment and provide a sense of safety and security. In such an environment, youngsters are freer to venture confidently, to meet new challenges, and to learn.

FOR CHILDREN

Learn how to express feelings. The ability to express feelings freely (in an acceptable way) adds a rich dimension to our lives. It opens up dialogue and provides grounds for a chance to grow. Not being in touch with our feelings can be very stressful. But not projecting feelings does not mean that they aren't there; feelings still function deep inside a person and come out indirectly. Do you know someone who is afraid to feel fear and so he comes across as angry? Or someone who is afraid to feel anger, so he seems scared? The ability to express one's feelings freely and appropriately is a very important skill. To be able to be close to someone and experience love and intimacy, you have to allow yourself to project feelings. We must all learn to feel our feelings, and to examine them, talk about them. This helps to discharge the energy around them—and in turn to reduce stress.

Learn how to receive and accept the "strokes" you need. All individuals need recognition. In addition, we all need to be nurtured, fondled, and "stroked" in order for our nervous systems to develop properly and for growth hormones from the pituitary gland to be produced sufficiently to let us develop. We never outgrow that need to be touched and nurtured. Our feelings of well-being and self-esteem are tied to it. In our culture we learn to substitute recognition—in the form of gestures, smiles, frowns, talk—for touching. We call that "stroking." However, we must learn to take responsibility for getting the strokes we need. In addition to communicating effectively in order to have our needs met, we must learn how to accept recognition—to let it soak in and freely revitalize us.

Part of being in charge of our lives and getting what we want (strokes and recognition) is learning to ask for and give strokes in a straightforward way. And part of being in charge of oneself is respecting other people's right to own themselves, too. They have a right to respond from their own selves. That may mean they may reject or refuse you. There are a variety of ways in which we can get our strokes, some better than others. They include:

• *Withdrawal.* We all need some time by ourselves, away from outside stimuli, to sort out our thoughts and get centered. We may leave the room physically to be by ourselves, or we may leave psychologically by screening out what is going on around us. Withdrawal may be the way we cope with stress or an unpleasant situation. Sometimes we copy the patterns that were effective for us in early childhood. When we withdraw, it is often into a world of pleasure or into creatively projecting "What if I were able to..." While withdrawal is the least productive way to get strokes, it can have the advantage of providing relaxation and avoiding overstimulation.

• *Rituals* are simply stereotyped transactions. They provide a safe way for people to be together since in these settings everybody knows what to do—what is expected of them and how to respond appropriately. Rituals offer a way to be with people without fear of rejection, and without having to be too close. These get-togethers usually make us feel good about ourselves.

- *Passing the time* talking about innocuous subjects (like the weather) is a safe way for people to learn about each other and see if they want to get to know each other better.
- *Activities* are structured time periods spent on something outside of us, such as work or sports. We may engage in activities because we want to, need to, or have to (like earning a living). We get strokes for performing or producing or from working well together. The strokes we get for what we *do* are good, but do not satisfy our need to be stroked for who we *are*.
- *Psychological games* provide strokes, help you prove you are right in the way you feel about yourself and others, and give you a payoff. However, while lending excitement, they often follow a predictable path and end with bad feelings for all the players.
- *Intimacy* is an opportunity for deep human contact. It brings out feelings of tenderness and caring in us. It also involves risk because it makes us vulnerable to rejection or fear of rejection. The feeling of being close to someone who knows all about us, with whom we don't have to pretend or wear a mask—being accepted for who we are—is the most precious stroke of all.

FOR PARENTS AND CHILDREN

Cultivate mental calmness. This can be achieved by working through three stages.

First, gather realistic information. You should become aware of the demands you will probably experience in a given situation. Get as much realistic information as you can, even if it's unpleasant information.

Second, when you begin to worry, get details of the resources available to you—resources that could help you cope more effectively with the situation. If there are no outside resources, then you should know that, too. You may be able to do something about it beforehand.

The final step is to encourage yourself to make plans to resolve the unpleasant or difficult situation and to reassure or reward yourself for doing so.

Draw vitality from stress. Experiencing stress is a fact of life. It is inevitable. But one of the positive aspects of stress is that, when recognized, it warns the body that something is wrong and gives us the chance to do something about it. To a degree, it is to everyone's advantage to seek some stress. It is possible to cultivate or improve your own talent for managing and utilizing stress. Here's how:

• *Make a conscientious effort to be an optimist.* It has been shown that stress-resistant people learn and practice a specific set of attitudes toward life—an openness to change; a feeling of commitment, enthusiasm, vitality, and involvement in whatever they do; and a sense of control over their lives. These attitudes have a profoundly positive effect on physiological and psychological health.

• *Turn problems into opportunities, and obstacles into creative solutions.* As you master problems, you gain confidence about your strengths, judgment, and resources. Generate several alternative solutions to problems.

• *Focus awareness and total concentration on the task at hand.* Completely immerse yourself in what you are doing. This allows you to respond totally to the immediate environment or task at hand.

• *Be adventuresome: Try something you thought you could never do.* Make this something you've always wanted to try, and entirely different from anything you have ever done before. Get involved in an exciting project.

• *Visualize yourself as vital and successful—a potential you.* You are the result of your image and beliefs. Concentrate on the qualities you want to possess.

Relieve tension with action. Participate in activities that help you release your pent-up emotions. Noncompetitive

exercise is an ideal energizer. Walking, swimming, danc-
ing, or other rhythmic body movements are excellent.
**Learn how to listen to the physical cues—warning signs—
that your body may be giving you.** Notice tension. Learn
how to relax your body.

**View constructive criticism as a means of self-improve-
ment. Don't allow criticism to intimidate or offend you
to the point of no action.** If you use it constructively as
opposed to taking it personally, criticism can help you
become all you can be.

Be aware of the importance of diet and nutrition. There
is no doubt that one's diet has a profound effect on one's
mental and physical well-being. Here are some basic
nutrition guidelines to follow:
  • Increase the consumption of fruits, vegetables, and whole
    grains.
  • Decrease overall food intake, if overweight, and begin
    exercising.
  • Decrease consumption of refined and processed sugars.
  • Decrease consumption of foods high in fats.
  • Decrease intake of salt and cholesterol. Resist peer pres-
    sure to smoke.
  • Avoid junk foods.
  • Resist pressure to drink. Learn to say "No, thanks."
  • Avoid caffeine. In excess it produces anxiety symptoms
    and it is addictive.
  • Avoid fad and quick-weight-loss diets. Long-term weight
    loss comes from regular exercise and good eating habits.
  • Decrease consumption of red meats and increase that
    of white meats and fish.
  • Eat smaller meals more frequently.

Cultivate an appreciation of self. Allow time for yourself.
You are responsible for preserving the "child" in you and
keeping that quest and zest for life alive. Slow down
enough to allow others an opportunity to appreciate what
is special about you. Your worth does not always depend
on how much you perform. Take time to reenergize—

to refill and replenish the senses. Don't be unnecessarily harsh with yourself. Avoid being a perfectionist; recognize areas of strength and weakness.

One of our fundamental roles as adults is to make certain that such basic, adaptive skills are taught by concerned, caring adults in the home, in the school, and in other learning environments. Another fundamental role is to nurture our young (as opposed to just rearing our kids). This nurturing becomes a function not only of the home and the school but of the entire social system. Recognizing that we are using our youngsters as scapegoats signals the need for a nurturing response.

The ability to cope successfully in the world is vital. It is our legacy to our children.

SEVEN

THE SCHOOL ENVIRONMENT

SCHOOL IS OFTEN NOT THE SAFE AND STIMULATING place in which we would wish our children to spend significant amounts of time. If we could design a perfect school (and home) environment, it would no doubt emphasize the following virtues—virtues that we spend our lives pursuing:

> *Identity.* A child needs to be considered a unique person in his or her own right, to be noticed and recognized as special. Each child needs to be given insight into recognizing and assessing his or her personal strengths and learning to compensate for weaknesses.
>
> *Belonging.* Every child needs to belong to someone or something, to be accepted and wanted.
>
> *Power.* Each child needs to achieve, to feel potent. To that end, children need flexibility to set their own goals and be in command of themselves.
>
> *Meaning.* All children need the events in their lives to add up to something. The meaning in children's lives adds

up to self-acceptance, self-esteem, high expectations, and hope for the future.

Change. Every child needs variety and positive change. Variety helps children avoid falling into ruts and helps them to grow continually.

Unfortunately, there is no perfect home or school environment, so parents and teachers have to do the best they can in nurturing children along these lines.

Children may not use sophisticated language in explaining school-related stresses, but if you ask why they feel bad, hostile, afraid or even sick, they can certainly tell you. School can and does represent criticism and rejection for many students. The source of criticism and rejection comes from other students, teachers, and support staff. If a school does not promote a safe and enriching learning environment, it can be deleterious to the emotional health of children.

In the school environment, students are most distressed when they fear another student and when school activities are not well supervised. Sadly, student violence escalates every year. According to a 1981 Senate subcommittee report, juvenile delinquency and violence continue to mount. Common incidents of such violence include verbal and physical threats, assault, rape, injury, theft, arson, and vandalism. At both high-school and college levels, weapons and drugs are prevalent. It is not unusual to find drugs, knives, and ammunition in a high-school student's locker. These factors together with the presence of gangs in the schools are a major source of anxiety and stress.

Between 1972 and 1978, classroom murders increased 18 percent, rape 40 percent, robberies 37 percent, and physical assault of teachers 77 percent. And these figures are still climbing. The annual destruction of school property exceeds $600 million. Ultimately, students feel they have to carry weapons in order to protect themselves from other students. Statistically, seventh graders are the most likely to be robbed or attacked, and ten-to-thirteen-year-olds are the highest risk group. Of these attacks and robberies, 42 percent are interracial. The smaller the minority group in a particular school, the more vulnerable that group is.

Students who are attacked without provocation or do not know their assailants—and the majority of assaults are of this type— experience the greatest prolonged levels of anxiety, stress, and depression. Students who have been victims of attack, robbery, or extreme verbal abuse are often likely to admit to being afraid on the way to or while in school. Also, they are more likely to dislike school and have low or below-average grades. If their uneasiness reaches the limit of tolerance, they will stay away from school.

Studies have shown that student stress is related to a number of school-specific factors that are in turn related to school crime, disorder, and aggression. Among these factors are the following:

Inadequate supervision
Crowded classrooms and schools
Ineffective teaching
Inappropriate curriculum
Forced integration

Inadequate Supervision

A student's risk of violent encounter is greatest during the time between classes. At these times, theft of money or possessions is most likely to occur. Of all thefts involving school-age victims throughout the nation, most happen during the school day. The dangerous sections of school buildings include crowded areas such as stairways, hallways, and cafeterias; areas off the beaten path such as storage rooms and unused classrooms; and areas where activities are supervised by only the students themselves.

Crowded Classrooms and Schools

Crowding contributes to violence and disruption because schools, particularly those in urban areas, are jammed with bigger pop- ulations than they were designed to serve. When the student population in a crowded school is reduced, there is a noticeable decline in violence and disruption. In addition, large schools have a higher incidence of serious crime than smaller schools. Students in smaller schools are more likely to be cooperative, since they identify with the school and their teachers, and are more likely to participate in school activities. This characteristic, which used to be called "school spirit," is difficult if not impossible to develop in large schools.

Ineffective Teaching/Inappropriate Curriculum

For the most part, the public assumes that a child's schooling begins with enrollment and ends with graduation. Many parents are not aware of all the variables that contribute to the potential stress of school-age children. Somehow, we have come to believe that the behavior of students can be understood only in terms of their role as learners. This is a mistake. We expect our children to be interested in and appreciative of a textbook education, but there is much more to their lives than school. Children, too, have expectations. Their preeminent concerns are *not* for studying and learning, but for socializing, security, attention, and evidence of self-worth.

Without these qualities, classrooms become places where anonymity, boredom, and anxiety are highly probable. In short, teachers must make deliberate efforts to provide for identity, stimulation, and security within the curriculum. In addition, teachers should remember the following:

- Children learn better when they are strongly motivated, not when they are regimented.
- Children learn in different ways, and it is important to find how a particular child can be helped to learn, rather than assume that there is only one method for all children.
- Children may experience roughly similar processes of development, but they do so at different times and different rates—a factor for which schools must adjust.
- In school, children learn a variety of attitudes and values that are as important as the basic skills. Teaching the basics must be attuned to enhancing these attitudes and values, which include honesty and fairness to others.

Forced Integration

For school integration to be successful, parents, teachers, administrators, and students alike must be committed to meeting the challenges and capitalizing on the advantages of a diversified student body. With many students in integrated schools sharing lockers, homework assignments, and participating in extracurricular activities with children from various races and ethnic backgrounds, it is important for parents and teachers to foster an understanding, acceptance, and appreciation of a diverse student population.

It is evident that a safe school is necessary for effective learning and efficient teaching. When the school environment is not safe, student stress becomes manifest. If such stress is severe, it leads to trauma. In such instances, children might suffer fatigue, weakness, blurred vision, irritability, dizziness, low morale, a sense of futility, or the equivalent of a generally depressed state.

Those students most susceptible to stress-related illnesses seem to have an impaired ability to deal effectively with fear or anger. Many students who succumb to sustained stress can be described as passive and rigid. These youngsters are unable to strike back when they find themselves the target of violence or hostility; instead, they internalize their fear or rage. Don't forget: Students do not receive formal psychological training that would prepare them for the threat of violence and abuse in school. Without preparation or training, many students are ill-equipped to confront the dangers endemic in their schools. Also, the normal response to danger is fear. Sustained incidences of the fear response can lead to hypertension, peptic ulcers, high blood pressure, asthma, diabetes, kidney disease, allergies, and other disorders. These are called "stress diseases" or "diseases of adaptation." The relationship of stress to physical illness is well documented. Further, when stress becomes unusually severe or chronic, it can lead to a psychiatric breakdown.

Any emotional upset can trigger a stress response and an accompanying physical disease. It is therefore not surprising that the expectation of a stressful event can be every bit as potent as the event itself. The way the child responds to the particular level of challenge depends on the following factors:

preparation
experience in stress management
sophistication in generating alternatives
success in finding the right coping technique

The effects of trauma and stress on children are based primarily on such factors as the severity of the conflict, the unexpectedness of the conflict, the chronic nature of the stimulus, the lack of good alternatives, and impaired morale. It is in these areas that parents and teachers can be of substantial help to children. Teachers deal with students every weekday and witness the surge of discipline problems, violence, verbal abuse, and vandalism that occurs during school hours. As teachers work to make schools safer and more conducive to learning, they can also publicize for parents the specific stresses children experience in the school environment.

A common outcome of stress in students is delinquency, and the traditional response to delinquency is suspension. However, this is rarely a deterrent or an effective treatment. A more successful approach would be to provide adequate psychological counseling or psychiatric help for troubled students. Unfortunately, this kind of counseling is not available in many schools. Nevertheless, parents and teachers can institute measures that would help children deal with stressful situations:

Preparedness. Psychological training to prepare students for stressful situations could minimize the impact of stress on students.

Morale. The opportunity for students to share their experiences with another person or group helps improve their morale.

Administrative Support. In schools where there is a high

profile of violence, disruption, or disorder, it is important that parents, educators, and students feel secure and have the support of the school and district administrators.

Expulsion. Students who have maliciously attacked fellow students, teachers, or staff members should not be allowed to return to the same school.

Reporting Violent Incidents. Students, parents, and teachers should have the opportunity to report directly to the school board concerning such issues as adverse school conditions, unfair administrators, overcrowding, violence, and severe disorder.

Crisis Intervention. A crisis-intervention team—whose function would be to defuse crises by implementing open-forum discussions at schools where teachers and students are involved in conflict—should be assigned to school districts.

Awareness and Commitment. Every effort should be made to alert parents and educators to the stress students encounter as well as to the impact of such stress on students.

School Responsibility. Good governance—a forgotten and newly rediscovered aspect of education—is expressed in school rules and regulations and is frequently found in formal social control and the importance placed on academic excellence, order, and an identification with the mission of the school. Evidence is abundant that school governance is a major factor determining the level of crime and disruption in schools.

Parent Involvement. Educators generally agree that the more active parents are in the educational process, the more effective the program for their children.

Improve Learning. Following are some suggestions for improvement in this area:

• Put more time, effort, and money into helping teachers contend with their task.
• Invest in the retraining of school principals.
• Enlist the community in understanding the learning and

teaching objectives of the school and in supporting the school.
- Improve the connection between learning research and existing classroom practices.
- Develop student records that will help schools to teach transient students more effectively.

Not everything a child learns in school is encompassed in the formal curriculum. An important part of a child's learning involves a healthy view of the world "out there." This kind of learning continues through a whole lifetime.

Students learn from the way the school is organized, the way teachers interact with students, and a host of other signals by which the school indirectly expresses its values. All these interactions not only demonstrate a wide range of personalities but also satisfy "people needs" like identity, belonging, power, meaning, and change.

On the following pages are charts to help you recognize the most likely sources of stress in your children as they progress through school, listed in order of their intensity for the youngsters.

KINDERGARTEN

STRESSOR	SIGNAL
1. Uncertainty + fear of abandonment by a significant adult.	1. References to this fear in nap and sleep; daydreaming; crying associated with parental absence; nail-biting.
2. Fear of wetting themselves.	2. Frequent trips to bathroom; occasional wetting; nail-biting; thumb-sucking; finger twirling in hair.
3. Fear of punishment/ reprimand from teacher.	3. The youngster will desire to please the teacher, but will be uncertain about how to do that, and fear that the teacher may not be pleased

or may even be angry. The child fears the teacher's response in expressing teacher disapproval.

FIRST GRADE

STRESSOR	SIGNAL
1. Fear of riding the bus.	1. Tries to persuade parents to drive him to school.
2. Fear of wetting in class.	2. Overly concerned; much time devoted to "what if" consequences; daydreaming and occasional wetting in class due to anxiety.
3. Teacher disapproval.	3. Continual seeking of teacher approval as opposed to more-independent action.
4. Ridiculed by class peers and older students in the school setting.	4. Child becomes "inward," expresses desire not to go to school.
5. Receiving first report card and not passing to second grade.	5. Higher frequency of negative self-talk—"I can't do it"—and low self-esteem.

SECOND GRADE

STRESSOR	SIGNAL
1. Frequently misses a particular parent.	1. Wants to go home/be with parent.
2. Fear of not being able to understand a given lesson (e.g., won't be able to spell words for tests, pass a test).	2. Inattention, crying, impatience with self.
3. Not being asked to be a "teacher helper."	3. Feels disliked by teacher; seeks *any* teacher attention, positive or negative.
4. Fear of teacher's discipline.	4. Refuses direct eye contact in a teacher-student activity.

5. Fear of being different from other children in dress and appearance.

5. Feels disliked by other children.

THIRD GRADE

STRESSOR

SIGNAL

1. Being chosen last on *any* team.

1. Verbal expression of not wanting to play "this stupid game"; being absent ("sick") on a given day.

2. Parent conference.

2. Failure to notify parent or take home notices; display of psychosomatic illness on this given day. The opposite extreme is evident in "perfect" behavior on that day.

3. Fear of peer disapproval and fear of not being liked by the teacher.

3. Complains about being excluded from favorite activities.

4. Fear of test taking and fear of not having enough time to complete work expectations on any and all test assignments (fear of failure to perform well).

4. Careless work; absence on a test day; task avoidance.

5. Staying after school.

5. Rushes to complete schoolwork; wants to make a commitment for getting picked up on certain days.

FOURTH GRADE

STRESSOR

SIGNAL

1. Being chosen last on *any* team.

1. Verbal expression of not wanting to play "this stupid game"; being absent ("sick") on a given day.

2. Peer disapproval of dress or appearance.

2. Will change clothes several times in the morning before reaching a decision on what they want (and intend!) to wear; hostility shown toward adult who selects that day's outfit.

3. Fear that a particular friend will select a different friend or share "their" secrets.

3. Jealously guards a friendship.

4. Fear of student ridicule.

4. Name-calling is "fair play."

5. Fear of not being personally liked by the teacher.

5. Wants to associate with the teacher.

FIFTH GRADE

STRESSOR

1. Being chosen last on *any* team.

SIGNAL

1. Verbal expression of not wanting to play "this stupid game"; being absent ("sick") on a given day.

2. Fear of losing "best friend" or that friend will share "secrets."

2. Jealously guards best friend.

3. Fear of being unable to complete schoolwork.

3. Procrastinates on task assignments; completes work carelessly.

4. Fear of peer disapproval.

4. Expects to select own clothing, own activities, own friends.

5. Fear of not being a "big sixth grader" next year.

5. Continually generates information / concerns on grades or "passing."

SIXTH GRADE

STRESSOR	SIGNAL
1. Being chosen last on *any* team.	1. Verbal expression of not wanting to play "this stupid game"; being absent ("sick") on a given day.
2. Fear of the unknown concerning own sexuality.	2. Shares gossip, myths, rumors, jokes concerning sexuality in all species.
3. Fear of not passing into middle school/junior high.	3. Renewed concentration on homework, or pronounced procrastination.
4. Fear of peer disapproval of appearance.	4. Renewed emphasis on appearance; experimentation with appearance (hair, clothes, etc.).
5. Fear of being unpopular.	5. Begins to select numerous friends but guards a selected friend (same sex).

SEVENTH GRADE

STRESSOR	SIGNAL
1. Fear of being selected first (and having to lead) and fear of being picked last (interpreted as being disliked or unpopular).	1. Exhibits extreme shyness or boldness; introvert or extrovert behavior becomes evident.
2. Fear of the unknown concerning own sexuality.	2. Shares gossip, rumors, myths concerning human sexuality; personal exploration and quest of facts concerning sexuality; careful observation of peers.
3. Extreme concern and worry	3. Exhibits little consistency

about emotional happiness and unhappiness (emotional fitness).

4. Fear of not being able to complete homework/schoolwork/task assignment.

5. Fear of school calling home.

in behavior; withdrawn, crowd-pleaser, loner, introvert, extrovert; periods of depression.

4. Perfectionism or procrastination.

5. Worries; is overly concerned; makes promises; is defensive.

EIGHTH GRADE

STRESSOR	SIGNAL
1. Fear of being selected first (and having to lead) and fear of being picked last (interpreted as being disliked or unpopular).	1. Exhibits extreme shyness or boldness; introvert or extrovert behavior becomes evident.
2. Fear of coming to terms with own sexuality (based on bits and pieces and lack of information concerning sex).	2. Serious exploration of facts and information concerning human sexuality, as well as examination of self as sexual being.
3. Extreme concern and worry about emotional happiness and unhappiness (emotional fitness).	3. Begins to reject feelings associated with being unhappy; avoids dealing with specific issues.
4. Fear of activities that require exposure of the body (phys. ed, etc.).	4. Occasionally absent from specific activities; feigns illness as avoidance; shows extreme shyness or crudeness regarding human sexuality.
5. Fear of being "the big ninth grader" but also of not passing into the ninth grade.	5. Tough, withdrawn, wants to know grades but may not utilize the information.

NINTH GRADE

STRESSOR	SIGNAL
1. Fear of coming to terms with sexuality (based on lack of information concerning sex).	1. Begins or continues sexual experimentation.
2. Fear of activities that require exposure of the body (phys. ed, etc.).	2. Occasionally absent from specific activities; feigns illness as avoidance; shows extreme shyness or crudeness regarding human sexuality.
3. Extreme concern and worry about emotional happiness and unhappiness (emotional fitness).	3. Begins or continues to reject feelings associated with being unhappy; avoids dealing with specific issues.
4. Fear of being sent to the assistant principal's office; confrontation with teacher; getting poor grades.	4. Embarrassment, cursing, panic, immediate compromise/cooperation; teacher-pleaser or overly defensive; periodic renewed interest in task commitment on a short-term basis.
5. Fear of being challenged to a confrontation by someone of the same sex.	5. Student-to-student confrontations; inability to use appropriate verbal communication and reasoning skills.

TENTH GRADE

STRESSOR	SIGNAL
1. Fear of being selected first (and having to lead) and fear of being picked last (interpreted as being disliked or unpopular).	1. Expresses unwillingness to participate.
2. Fear that another peer will	2. Jealously guards relation-

vie for their "sweetheart" (significant relationship).

3. Personal fear of not having felt or derived a significant or positive meaning from schooling ("I feel I take school too lightly—so many subject areas are just not interesting to me"; "I don't do well in school, but I don't know why").

4. Fear of participating in athletics and failing; of participating in clubs, organizations, or school projects and not being popular or selected for specifics.

5. Fear of not completing class assignments.

6. Fear of getting caught cheating.

7. Questions family relationships/family interpersonal relationship.

ship; tendency toward fighting in such confrontations.

3. Expresses negative self-concept.

4. Limited or lack of participation.

5. Cheating.

6. Denial, defensiveness, cursing.

7. "Tunes out" family relationships as "insigificant" at this time; defensive toward authority.

ELEVENTH GRADE

STRESSOR

1. Fear of undressing in a group.

2. Fear of being "not OK"/ridiculed in class when asked to speak or demonstrate.

3. Fear that peers will negatively view the physical self (fat, skinny legs, ugly, etc.).

SIGNAL

1. Introspective.

2. Interpretation of physical self and coming to terms (being honest) about realities.

3. Seeks confirmation about being "OK."

4. Fear of inadequate vocational or academic training.

4. Expresses confusion as to career options and/or interests in job/career/role selection.

5. Fear of not having enough money.

5. Seeks jobs; steals.

6. Fear of sexual expression ("How do others view me sexually?").

6. Heavy experimentation or total withdrawal in seeking or maintaining personal relationships with the opposite sex.

7. Fear that other adults will interpret roles for them. (They seek to define themselves in relation to peers and own values and goals.)

7. Hostility toward authority and toward many adult groups; easily put on the defensive.

TWELFTH GRADE

STRESSOR

SIGNAL

1. Fear that other adults will interpret roles for them. (They seek to define themselves in relation to peers and own values and goals.)

1. Hostility toward authority and toward many adult groups; easily put on the defensive.

2. Fear of inadequate vocational or academic training.

2. Expresses confusion as to career options and/or interests in job/career/role selection.

3. Fear of lack of readiness past graduation.

3. Appears irresponsible in decisions and actions.

4. Fear of not having enough money.

4. Seeks and holds jobs (sometimes two).

5. Fear that preoccupation with self-needs (physical, job, career, personal, peer, ego) results in deficiency in school role as a "learner."

5. Defensive ("Why do we have to do this dumb stuff anyway?"); fails to take an active interest unless activities prove "relevant for me."

Remember, when a youngster exhibits one or even more than one of these behaviors, it does not necessarily mean an unhealthy, stressful condition—but the likelihood that there is something seriously wrong is strong, so be alert! And use your common sense: You know your child better than anyone.

PART III

ENVIRONMENTAL FACTORS AND STRESS

EIGHT

DISEASE AND ENVIRONMENTAL IMBALANCE

IS THERE A LINK BETWEEN ENVIRONMENTAL CON-
tamination and the deterioration of children's overall health? Is
the increasing onset of disease, illness, and stress related to such
contamination?

While these and similar questions require considerable investigation, experts agree that escalating environmental pollutants
play a crucial role and are in fact reflected in the sharp rise of
these and other conditions.

One of the most widespread diseases—cancer—is now the
leading cause of natural death in youngsters under the age of
fifteen, preceded only by traumatic accidents such as death by
fire. Two decades ago, childhood cancer was such a rarity that
cases were recorded in medical journals. Now an increasing number of children succumb to Hodgkin's disease and other lym-
phomas and osteogenic sarcomas. Indeed, childhood cancer is
so common that almost everyone can cite a case within his or
her group of friends or acquaintances.

Several decades ago, Dr. Frances Pottenger experimented on

the effect of diets on the health of animals. She selected various groups of animals and fed raw milk and raw meat to half of the animals in her study, and cooked meat and pasteurized milk to the other half. Initially the difference in diet had little effect on either their health or longevity. With each successive generation, however, Pottenger observed progressive deterioration in the group fed cooked meat and pasteurized milk, whereas those fed the raw diet continued to demonstrate a greater resistance to disease and illness and appeared to have greater stamina, vitality, and general health. The first evidence of trouble in the former group was a rising incidence of problems with reproduction: repeated miscarriages and long and difficult labors. Other signs of distress surfaced: The animals' coats became rough and dull, instinctive maternal habits began to deteriorate, and there was a greater range in temperament and emotional adjustment. By the fifth generation, the group fed a cooked diet was reportedly so "high strung and vicious" that special protective equipment was required while handling the animals. The next generation showed skeletal malformations, and by the ninth generation they were completely unable to reproduce.

Pottenger also discovered that in the outdoor pens of those animals fed the raw diet, the foliage was greener, and that crops planted in these pens outproduced those planted in the pens of the animals on a cooked diet. She concluded that this is an important ecological principle.

While there is certainly a big difference between the metabolism of animals and humans, Pottenger's study does demonstrate that the quality of nutrition in one generation has powerful effects upon those that follow. Are we witnessing a similar, large-scale experiment, but with human beings as the subjects in the study? In a sense we are all guinea pigs in a vast trial-and-error experiment on the effects of our modern forms of food. There are few if any precedents for current agricultural, dietary, and ecological practices.

Ever since we discovered that the large quantities of nitrogen, phosphorus, and potassium left over from World War II wartime explosives industries could be used as fertilizer to produce enormous crop yields, agriculture has never been the same. Fertilizing farm crops is now radically different from the traditional practices. Chromium, manganese, nickel, molybdenum, germanium, selenium, and iron are vital to the human metabolism, yet my father, an agricultural farmer for nearly four decades, maintains that our topsoil has become progressively depleted of these minerals each year. Experts concur. Now it has become necessary to create more and better hybrid strains of plants that can adapt to chemical fertilizers. But because these strains, in many respects, are weaker than the original strain, we soon discover that these plants are more and more susceptible to insects, fungi, and even weak overgrowth. To combat this, we have responded by creating powerful insecticides, fungicides, and herbicides, all synthesized from petroleum and all toxic to animal and human life. In turn, these chemicals have upset the delicate ecological balance of topsoil: They have wiped out earthworms and many of the necessary soil bacteria.

Are our agribusiness practices affecting the health of either this or future generations? Besides the imbalance of our nutritional diets, we must also contend with air and water pollutants. Dr. Henry Schroeder has alerted us to the major metabolic stress caused by heavy-metal toxicity. In addition, we are exposed daily to increasing levels of radioactive pollution, carbon monoxide, and other deadly fumes and airborne particles.

We have been forewarned, but to little avail. In the early Fifties, Rachel Carson warned us about modern agribusiness in her book *The Silent Spring*; *Consumer Beware* by Beatrice Trum Hunter presented the dangers of food processing; and Frances Moore Lappe, in her classic *Diet for a Small Planet*, educated us about growing food for dietary balance.

Allergies

Dr. Theron Randolph was one of the first scientists to identify processed foods as the cause of chronic allergic syndromes, which in turn resulted in stress. In some people, foods rarely eaten can provoke acute reactions. Such a reaction is called an "unmasked food sensitization."

"Masked" food allergies are caused by certain foods commonly eaten which when withdrawn produce an adverse reaction—an addiction. To discover whether a person has a masked food addiction, clinical ecologists will subject the person to a three-to-twelve-day denial of the food in question. If the person experiences withdrawal reactions, food allergy is suspected. Once the test period is completed, suspected foods are given in separate feedings to discover which food(s) caused the withdrawal symptoms.

The fact that allergic reactions can cause violent behavior is considered a recent phenomenon, related to our highly processed modern diet, as allergies are almost never seen in people living a primitive life-style, eating a natural diet. The typical modern diet, high in nonnutritive sugar and refined foods, does not provide optimal nutrition and therefore lowers resistance to allergies.

Psychiatrists, allergists, and other physicians have been successfully treating patients with behavioral problems by identifying offending foods and chemicals in their environment. One of the earliest cases was reported by Dr. B. R. Hoobler in 1916 when he identified infants sensitive to proteins. Studies since then have suggested that adverse reactions to foods can be one of the causes of hyperactivity, nervousness, stealing, learning problems, minimal brain dysfunction, depression, hostility, aggression, irritability, stress, and periods of confusion.

Many foods have been found to be major causes of children's stress-related behavior problems. The primary offenders are soft drinks, cake, cookies, candy, ice cream, and sugared cereals. When these are removed from a youngster's diet, their behavior improves significantly.

Disease

The U.S. Government Health Agency, the Vital and Health Statistics, and other health agencies all report that chronic diseases and illnesses among U.S. youngsters are on the rise. What is perhaps even more startling is that many of these chronic diseases, along with subtle psychological changes in temperament, are stress-related.

Obviously, something is seriously wrong. Stress-related chronic diseases and illnesses among children in America, the most affluent country in the world, are at an all-time high at a time when we would assume that these factors in our young population would be diminishing. But even with the advances in medical science and the steady proliferation of programs designed to heighten our awareness of and commitment to the well-being of children, we find they are not. In fact, their rate of incidence is sharply rising.

As we had hoped, the rate of communicable diseases of early childhood has fallen off dramatically, and infectious diseases, formerly major health hazards, are at an all-time low. This is due in part to new therapeutic procedures, improved sanitation, and advances in immunology. Data from HEW, Health and Environment, support evidence of a 144-percent decrease in the death rate for children from influenza and pneumonia in the last forty-five years. The accompanying table depicts leading causes of deaths among American children as well as the rate of change between 1900 and 1970.

CAUSES OF DEATH	RATES PER 100,000		PERCENT OF CHANGE
	1900	1970	
Tuberculosis (all forms)	195	3	99 better
Influenza and Pneumonia	202	31	85 better
Major Cardiovascular Diseases	345	494	43 worse
Malignant Neoplasms (Cancer)	64	162	153 worse

Even with the decline in incidence of acute disease, *more* youngsters are susceptible to a *greater* number of diseases and illnesses. The rate of heart disease among American children is now the highest in the world, with asthma ranking as the second most prevalent chronic condition among children. Following in order, youngsters in the U.S. suffer from impairments of the lower extremities, mental and nervous conditions, and psychosocial abnormalities.

There are now numerous cases of babies born with malignancies; and cardiovascular diseases and birth defects have almost tripled in the last twenty-five years. Chronic disease and illness for U.S. youngsters increases with age: ten-to-sixteen-year-olds are most frequently affected. In 1967 nearly 25 percent of youngsters under the age of sixteen suffered from one or more chronic diseases or illnesses, an increase of nearly 6 percent over the previous decade. Nearly 15 percent of the eighteen-year-olds were rejected by Selective Service in 1965 because of conditions due to childhood disease and related illnesses. Physicians report that many of these conditions could have been alleviated had they been treated in childhood. According to the National Health Survey's study, one youngster out of every ten is reported to have serious allergic conditions, and asthma is the primary cause of school absences for young children.

Of particular significance in regard to the increased rate of chronic disease and illness among the young is the fact that there has been an increase in the number of youngsters experiencing stress. Deaths due to ulcers have risen sharply among fifteen-to-twenty-four-year-olds, and are continuing to rise. Thus far, modern medicine has not been successful in preventing ulcer deaths among either very young children or those in the fifteen-to-twenty-four-year-old age category. Experts in several fields have attributed this ineffectiveness to the increase in psychological and physiological stress experienced by children. Even more dramatic are recent reports on the increase of deaths among newborn infants as a result of ulcers. And such ulcers are almost invariably linked to stress. Whatever the cause, more and more youngsters are ill more and more often, and their illness is more often than not stress-related.

NINE

DIET AND STRESS

LESS THAN THIRTY-FIVE YEARS AGO, A HYPERAC-
tive child was a rarity. Today it is difficult to find someone in
North America who doesn't know a hyperactive child. The incidence of hyperactivity paired with learning disability is higher
in the United States than in any other country of the world. And
delinquency is on the rise too. In 1978, over 12 million children
under the age of eighteen were arrested for crimes other than
traffic violations. In 1979, over a million children were placed
in detention centers for some period of time. Could the way we
eat contribute to these problems?

As a matter of record, diet can profoundly affect emotional
stability and adaptability to stress. The effect of alcohol and drugs
on our stability is well documented. Now the stress relationship
of diet to delinquency and crime is under careful scrutiny. It is
currently believed that food can alter our state of mind in much
the same way as alcohol and drugs.

Over 50 percent of the average American's diet consists of
processed food. Over 4,000 additives can be found in the Amer-

ican food supply, none of which have been thoroughly tested for their effect on our central nervous systems. We have become a nation of fast-food junkies, coffee and cola drinkers, and refined-carbohydrate fanatics. It is time to take stock of the debilitating influence of all this junk food on our children.

How does diet influence state of mind and emotional balance? The brain is no different than the rest of the body. Brain cells require proper feeding in order to function correctly. In point of fact, the brain is the body's most chemically sensitive organ. Deprived of proper nutrients or overwhelmed by toxic pollutants, the brain cannot perform at peak efficiency. Though it is traditional to explore psychological and socioeconomic factors for answers to delinquent behavior in children, new research suggests that metabolic disorders or inadequate nutrition can contribute significantly to antisocial behavior.

Recent studies indicate that too much sugar, vitamin deficiencies, lead pollution, and food allergies can seriously disrupt the brain's ability to function normally and effectively. Criminologists, who have largely ignored biochemical influences as a possible cause of criminal behavior in children, are now rethinking that connection. This new concern with biochemical factors is dramatically changing the way juvenile authorities and the courts are treating juvenile crime. For instance, in South Dakota several years ago, it was found that the group homes that served a better diet to the youngsters had better results in rehabilitating them. When they ate fresh vegetables and were not given caffeine or processed sugar, and exercised daily, they were better able to behave normally. In Illinois similar results were reported.

Several years ago, the San Luis Obispo Juvenile Probation Department in California established a clinical Ecology Treatment Program to work with difficult juvenile offenders. They were tested for biochemical imbalances and nutritional habits, and it was discovered that they all had severe "body-chemistry imbalances." When dietary change was instituted, the success of the program was overwhelming. Children experiencing a high degree of stress showed the following symptoms:

Anxiety
Blurred vision
Craving for alcohol
Craving for sweets
Depression
Dizziness, faintness
Feelings of doom
Headaches
Insomnia, nightmares

Irritability
Morning nausea
Nervousness
Rage
Temporary muscle aches
Temporary pain in joints
Tiredness, weakness
Weight problems

The researchers found that the typical diet for these children consisted of the following:

No breakfast or a breakfast high in sugar
Skipped meals
Light eating during the day
Heavy eating at night
Refined carbohydrates for snacks

As well, they found a heavy consumption of

Alcohol
Caffeine
Junk food
Packaged (not fresh) foods

Salt
Sugar
Tobacco
White flour

In light of this study, it seems clear that dietary counseling must become a mandatory part of school programs, and that parents must learn the fundamentals of good nutrition for their children. Several experts have developed a diet for youngsters who experience high levels of stress or who are continual substance abusers:

• Eat at least three, evenly spaced, well-balanced meals each day.

- Consume adequate protein daily, whether animal or vegetable. (The rule of thumb to determine your child's protein need is to divide his or her body weight by two. The number reached represents the number of protein grams your child needs every day.)
- Consume fresh fruits and vegetables daily.
- Use only whole grains.
- Include legumes and nuts in the diet.
- Use sparingly salt, dried fruits, coffee, tea, or tobacco.
- Allow a fruit, vegetable, or protein snack between meals or before your child's bedtime.

Foods to be avoided are

Alcohol	Fruit-flavored drinks
Breakfast cereals, commercially made granola	Honey, molasses
	Ice cream
Cakes	Pastries
Candy	Pies
Canned fruit	Processed or packaged food
Canned vegetables	Soft drinks
Coffee	Sugar—white, brown, turbinado, raw
Cookies	
Corn syrup	Tea
Doughnuts	White bread
Flavored yogurt	White flour

These excellent dietary suggestions reduce or eliminate most additives, lower consumption of refined carbohydrates, and provide essential vitamins and minerals. Because of the connection between nutrition and stress behavior, it is imperative that parents and schools provide sufficient nutrition for children.

Here are dietary goals established by the U.S. government:

1. To avoid overweight, consume only as many calories as are expended. If overweight, decrease caloric consump-

tion and increase physical activity.

2. Increase the intake of complex carbohydrates and "naturally occurring" sugars from about 28 percent to about 48 percent of total calories consumed.

3. Reduce the intake of refined and processed sugars to account for no more than 10 percent of total caloric consumption.

4. Reduce overall fat intake from approximately 40 percent to about 30 percent of caloric consumption.

5. Reduce saturated-fat intake to account for about 10 percent of total caloric consumption. Balance it with polyunsaturated and monounsaturated fats, each of which should also account for about 10 percent of caloric consumption.

6. Reduce cholesterol consumption to about 300 milligrams a day.

7. Limit the intake of sodium by reducing the intake of salt to about five grams a day.

The goals suggest the following changes in food selection and preparation:

1. Increase consumption of fruits, vegetables, and whole grains.

2. Decrease consumption of refined and other processed sugars and foods high in such sugars.

3. Decrease consumption of foods high in total fat, and partially replace saturated fats, whether obtained from animal or vegetable sources, with polyunsaturated fats.

4. Decrease consumption of animal fat, and choose meats, poultry, and fish that will reduce saturated-fat intake.

5. Except for young children, substitute low-fat and nonfat milk for whole milk, and low-fat dairy products for high-fat dairy products.

6. Decrease consumption of butterfat, eggs, and other high-cholesterol foods. Some consideration should be given to easing the low cholesterol goal for premenopausal

women, young children, and the elderly in order to obtain the nutritional benefits of eggs in the diet.

7. Decrease consumption of salt and of foods with a high salt content.

Breakfast must not be missed, and should preferably consist of fruits and grains, which will steadily release glucose during the day, giving fuel to the brain.

One of the best ways in which a parent can help a child avoid stress is to provide him or her with a balanced diet that includes all the components necessary to good physical *and* thus good mental health.

TEN

SOUND AND STRESS

THERE IS A DIRECT RELATIONSHIP OF SOUND TO stress or *dis*-stress. We live in an ocean of sound. The individual sounds in this ocean exert a tremendous influence on our physical and psychological state of being. Our bodies resonate automatically in response to the sounds that surround us. While some sounds can keep us well and "in tune" with ourselves, some sounds can make us literally ill. The notion that it is possible to harness the positive forces and energies of sound to create health (physical and psychological harmony and balance) and, conversely, minimize the negative effects of harsh and unnatural sound vibration merits attention.

Because our modes of perception are visually oriented for the most part, we tend to take for granted, ignore, or block out many of the sounds in our environment. While this is certainly necessary for sanity if not survival, we do know that certain levels of harsh environmental sound pollution are nonetheless extremely harmful.

Radionics is the study of vibrations and their relationship to the health and vigor of the body, particularly the muscles and organs. Dr. Hans Jenny has photographed the incredible patterns formed by sound, demonstrating the effect that "invisible" sound has on the body, and Itzhak Bentov has been able to measure micromotion in the body. All research verifies that sounds resonate in different parts of the body. It is believed that low-register tones resonate in the lower parts of the body, middle-register tones resonate in the chest cavity, and high tones localize in the head area. Philosophers from Plato and Pythagoras to Gurdjieff used mantras and chants for physical healing and emotional well-being. The power of music to influence certain body parts and to activate specific energy centers has been recorded far back in history.

Music: The Relaxational Response

Recent research concludes that highly relaxing and meditative music produces a significant alteration in brain waves that evokes a healing response. These recent studies differ significantly from earlier studies that focused on either physical responses (such as pulse rate) or psychological responses (the responses of emotion). These recent studies also provide further evidence of the entire physical and electromagnetic energy structure of the body as opposed to the duality of the mind/body conceptualization.

The National Music Therapy Association concurs, offering a catalog that lists highly relaxing, meditative, soothing music. One important distinction should be noted: An individual may intellectually follow music and *assume* it to be relaxing even though the body is not perceiving it to be so. Deep relaxation occurs at the physiological and psychological level: Breathing is slowed; heartbeat is more regular; the mind is soothed. The body is at peace with itself. Researchers now believe that the music stimulus is assimilated by the entire body at the cellular level and can be enhanced by the use of color. By correlating the seven musical tonal centers and the seven rainbow colors with the seven longer and lasting etheric energy centers in the human body, a deeper and longer-lasting response is achieved. Color research has expanded our concept of the impact of color: We now know that colors, too, have areas of resonance in both the body and psyche. Music can nourish the body. It has a great potential to create a state of ease, but it can also create a state of dis-ease. We are becoming more and more aware of the power of sound in our lives. *It is necessary to help youngsters share the aural programming in their own environments.* Why is this important? Sound, like light, is nothing more than pure energy. Music resonance is vibrational energy and is assimilated at the cellular level within the body. As such it has the capacity to affect mood greatly. While the ear gets credit for being the major pathway for aural processing, there is evidence that the entire body serves as a receptor for sound—even when the mind is not consciously processing the incoming information. The work of numerous researchers has proved that whether you hear a sound consciously or not, your body not only hears the vibration but responds to it at the cellular level.

In Europe and other parts of the world, the science of radionics has progressed to using induced sound vibrations as treatment for malfunctioning internal organs. Pure vibrations, via a tone-frequency generator, are transduced directly into the skin, allowing the body to assimilate needed energy patterns. Organs and muscles in a state of dis-ease are quickly restored to balance since the incoming vibration complements the actual calculated vibration rates of the organ and enhances its vitality. If someone has a malfunctioning liver, instead of being given drugs, the patient receives a portion of sound vibrations to restore the liver's functioning capacities. Sophisticated research already exists on correlating specific sound vibrations with the structure and functioning of each internal organ.

Much of the music in our industrial age is not conducive to harmonious inner well-being. Disco music, for example, consists mainly of loud drums and lower-chakra resonances. The actual mix of the music overemphasizes the drum and electric-bass volume, allowing it to take precedence over melody and harmony. Rock music actually produces inner dis-ease by disturbing the inner balance of the body rhythm. Even the monotonous tone of television has a negative impact on the nervous system.

Choosing background music should be a conscious decision. It has been found that appropriate background music in learning environments can greatly enhance the learning process. Imbalance can actually be viewed as a physical sensation signaling that one's inner system is not working in harmony with one's outer processes. Becoming more familiar with and sensitive to our inner rhythms will help us become more effective in protecting our moods and health.

Youngsters, Sound, and Stress: Considerations

Authorities have established that there are correlative physiological reactions to our emotional responses to sounds. This knowledge of chemical and electrical coordinates is so widely accepted in the music industry that it is being used to dictate which tunes will be released and to predict which ones will become hits. One of the most successful rhythm sounds uses the drumbeat to stimulate the beat of the human heart. Much of pop music is built around a bass drumbeat. It is felt that both soft and hard rock produce physiological and psychological tension and contribute to stress since the beat is counter to the human heartbeat. The research of Dr. Sheldon Deal, a nationally known chiropractor and author, produces evidence that the "short-short-long" (as opposed to the natural "long-short-short" rhythm used by the American Indians) beat of rock music has a definite weakening effect on muscle strength.

The electrical changes that occur while listening to music also manifest themselves on the surface of the skin. They can therefore be measured by the same kind of biofeedback apparatus used in lie detectors.

Because our stimulation by certain kinds of sounds can be easily predicted, we are witnessing more and more scientific applications of psychoacoustics—as in commercials, where the selection of background sounds and rhythms are carefully calculated for their emotional impact.

The Stress Connection

Where there is disharmony, there is dis-ease. It appears that in our modern-day society, bombarding sounds create a great deal of physiological and psychological dis-ease. The findings of numerous studies show that noise can have a negative effect on your mental health. Admissions to mental hospitals were 29 percent higher in the area where the Los Angeles airport is located than in other local areas that are racially, economically, and socially similar. London's Heathrow Airport area showed a 31-percent higher admission rate than other, similar areas. Furthermore, studies have shown that workers in professions where harsh sounds abound have a higher incidence of cardiovascular disease, headaches, and respiratory disorders. And people subjected to this increased noise experience increased anger, frustration, and overall stress.

If sound produces stress, can it also help to alleviate it?

Sounds for Well-Being: What to Do

Various professional people, appliance manufacturers, city planners, health facilities, schools, and restaurants are now considering ways in which the positive potential of musical sound vibrations can minimize the effect of sound pollution and maximize the environment and the "attunement" of that music for humans in a given environment. There are now music specialists who design background music environments attuned to the human use of particular settings, such as hospitals, clinics, schools, movie theaters, and restaurants.

Dr. Steven Halpern has become best known for his extraordinary efforts in this area. The "Spectrum Suite" sound track that has been used over the last few years, for example, has been found to be effective in establishing health-supportive environments. The overall efficiency of the body system is increased and bodily functions are enhanced by utilizing the seven notes of the musical octave in tandem with the seven colors of the visual spectrum and seven chakras to bring all of the body's major energy centers into attunement. "Starborn Suite," a lyrical, flowing motif featuring piano, organ, and violins, evokes serene images and mood transformations. *Eastern Peace* is a definitive expression of the inner impact of Eastern and Western musical modalities, utilizing eternal harmonies that underlie all music. Piano, bamboo flute, and tamboura accompaniment is highlighted. "Ancient Echoes" is a vocal arrangement featuring the flute and harp for deep relaxation. "Trance Dance" explores avenues of emotional expression, while "Here to Eternity," featuring Middle Eastern percussion, temple bells, flutes, tamboura, and ocean guitar, enhances the effects of meditation and massage. "Rain Ragas" features traditional and improvisational contexts supporting the idea that the language of music is truly universal.

So that sound can be most beneficial in your life:

- Be aware of what background music is being selected.
- When purchasing home or office appliances, select those that are quiet-running. Further reduce their sound by positioning them on or near sound-deadening materials (rubber, felt, sound-absorbent fiber glass, etc).
- Learn to appreciate and respect your own integrity and your right to privacy from sounds that create dis-ease.
- Learn to moderate the sounds you yourself make.
- Learn how to adapt to sounds you cannot change. The hum of your car motor, for example, can be offset by converting it into a more soothing image of a flowing ocean, or soften it with the low hum of your own voice, or programmed music.

PART IV

THE DARKER SIDE OF STRESS

ELEVEN

DRUG AND VITAMIN ABUSE

CHILDREN STRUGGLE TO BALANCE THE COMPETing priorities of school, work, social life, and other essential life experiences. Still, no matter how fast they run, there are only twenty-four hours in every day. So children often depend on a wide variety of methods to squeeze more productivity from each day. Some listen to tapes while sleeping or review lecture notes while jogging or have a study date with a girlfriend or boyfriend or operate on less sleep. Or take stimulants.

The kinds of stimulants available to children are numerous, from caffeine (in coffee, tea, cola, No-Doz, etc.) to diet pills, amphetamines, and cocaine. Students rely on such stimulants for increased alertness, a sense of well-being, and stamina for prolonged or physically strenuous tasks. Unfortunately, stimulants also drastically undermine children's health.

To begin with, stimulants do not enhance complex intellectual functions. If a student takes stimulants to increase an intellectual skill he just doesn't possess, the student is only fooling himself. Any possible academic assistance from stimulants is marginal, fleeting at best. Staying awake all night is decidedly inferior to getting a good night's sleep and may actually diminish a child's performance. Using stimulants to stay awake has an adverse effect on studying. By depriving himself or herself of sleep, a child actually decreases intellectual effectiveness and testing ability. Excessive use of stimulants can also lead to anxiety, paranoia, depression, aggression, and even violence. In addition, stimulants may increase the pulse rate, raise blood pressure, and influence the heartbeat. In fact, high doses of caffeine alone can produce symptoms indistinguishable from those of anxiety neuroses. Agitation, nervousness, irritability, headaches and high blood pressure can occur with the fifteen to seventy-five milligrams of mild stimulants found in many diet pills. With higher doses of amphetamines (ten to twenty milligrams), the child experiences not only nervousness, headaches, and high blood pressure, but paranoia, extreme aggressiveness, and hallucinations. The same symptoms that occur with amphetamines occur with cocaine.

The most obvious ingredient in good study habits is common sense. A child can profitably schedule a certain number of study hours each day and discipline himself to study on a regular basis. If no procrastination is allowed, there will never be a danger of needing to cram or to stay up all night. A student should have between six and eight hours of sleep a night. In fact, students should be encouraged to develop regular sleep and relaxation habits to accompany their study habits. These sound, regular habits will help them to be better organized, more relaxed, and better prepared for classes.

Megavitamins are also being abused by students who have interpreted the benefits of vitamins and minerals as an antidote for several conditions, including drug and alcohol abuse, poor nutrition, and inadequate rest. Each year millions of students overdose on megavitamins. Indeed, students are so misinformed about vitamins that parents have reason to fear the effects of megavitamin abuse, especially in high-school students. Students are often taking 100 times the government-recommended dosages. Massive amounts of vitamins are not only ineffective, they are unsafe. Vitamin enthusiasts contend that large doses of certain vitamins will do everything from curing the common cold to preventing cancer. For school, they claim the benefits include sharpening the mind and senses, compensating for lost sleep, and helping students cope with the stress and strains of adolescence. The straight talk on megavitamins is short: *No one needs them.* Along with proteins, carbohydrates, and fats, the human body needs vitamins—not megavitamins—and minerals to function properly. Vitamins are organic substances that are often not manufactured by our bodies. Vitamins help us convert food into tissue and help us utilize the energy in food. Minerals are inorganic compounds that contribute to energy production and body maintenance. Researchers are still unsure about how minerals and some vitamins interact and specifically contribute to health. However, there is growing emphasis on the importance of interaction between vitamins and minerals. It has been found that the essential transfer of nutrients from food to the body is influenced by many variables, such as the physiological makeup of the individual, his diet, and the types and quality of food consumed. Because balance among nutrients is crucial, it is necessary to be cautious about taking huge amounts of any vitamin or mineral. It should be emphasized that while vitamin and mineral supplements may be beneficial, they will not compensate for poor nutrition.

When the body takes in more vitamins than it requires, the excess may have negative side effects. For instance, fat-soluble vitamins—A, D, E, and K—are stored in body fat, and the accumulation of very large doses can cause illness. A large helping of vitamin D does not make bones superstrong; what it may do is cause kidney damage, extreme fatigue, and loss of appetite. Water-soluble vitamins—B and C—dissolve in water, so for the most part the body simply excretes what it doesn't need in urine and perspiration. But researchers have recently begun to uncover side effects of large doses of water-soluble vitamins.

It is beneficial and necessary to separate vitamin myth from reality. For more than a decade, internationally known chemist and Nobel Prize winner Linus Pauling has been promoting large doses of vitamin C as a protection against the common cold, flu, and a host of other ailments. The recommended daily allowance (RDA) for vitamin C is sixty milligrams for adults, but Dr. Pauling recommends daily doses of 1,000 to 5,000 milligrams to prevent a cold, and as much as 15,000 milligrams a day to cure one.

More than 2 million Americans reportedly believe in the powers of vitamin C. There is some evidence that large doses of vitamin C may act as a mild antihistamine, but whether it is worthwhile to take large doses of vitamin C for 365 days in order to achieve a mild antihistaminic effect during the eight days out of an entire year the average person has a cold is certainly doubtful. Megadoses of vitamin C are not harmless; as little as ten times the RDA (i.e., 600 milligrams) taken over a period of time can produce gout in people predisposed to the disease as well as an increased susceptibility to kidney stones. Megadoses of C can also cause false responses in tests such as those used by diabetics to check their sugar levels and in stool tests used to screen for cancer of the colon.

In a new and alarming development, megadoses of vitamin C were found to be destructive to vitamin B-12. Since vitamin C is acidic, it destroys B-12 when the two are mixed in a test tube. While it is difficult to measure what happens inside the body, we do know that a lack of B-12 can cause a type of anemia, severe brain damage, and even death.

Should you take megadoses of vitamin C to protect yourself against disease? On balance, the known risks outweigh the proven benefits. But now that there is an indication that vitamin C is somehow involved with the immune system—at least in guinea pigs—it makes sense to have adequate sources of C in your diet, especially if you are prone to infections. We can easily get the RDA of vitamin C naturally, from fruits and vegetables. Whether vitamin C has the ability to provide a healthy, cold-free year is questionable according to a special Department of Agriculture report on human nutrition. It takes a wide range of proteins, minerals and vitamins—including A, B-1, B-6, and E, in addition to C—to produce the antibodies needed to resist and recover from disease.

There is no known diet that will prevent cancer, but there is growing evidence that the lack of certain vitamins and minerals may be related to tumor growth. For example, vitamin A deficiency is related to cancer of the colon and salivary gland; chronic B-12 deficiency to cancer of the esophagus; and gross deficiencies of iodine to thyroid and breast cancer. Since tumors that spread to other parts of the body are responsible for more than 90 percent of all cancer deaths, scientists have been increasingly exploring the relationship between vitamins and cancer.

Thus far there is no documented link between megadoses of vitamins or minerals and cancer. Large doses of vitamins will neither prevent nor cure it. Even a cancer related to the lack of a certain vitamin cannot be prevented by taking in more vitamins than the body can absorb. However, because vitamin A is involved in controlling the normal growth of cells—and cancer occurs when this process is out of control—researchers have been particularly interested in it.

Vitamin E is most commonly abused by students who contend that it will offset damage due to excessive drinking. Based on pure assumption, thousands of high-school students overdose on E, thinking it offsets the long-term effects of alcohol on the body. Vitamin E is also a popular anti-aging remedy, and although it has never been proved to influence human reproduction, it has also been heralded as a way to prevent male impotence or sterility. Excess vitamin E can cause nausea, leg cramps, intestinal disorders, blurred vision, and a critical interference with the ability of the blood to clot normally.

Many high-school students falsely believe that massive doses of vitamin D taken before examinations or competitive events will make them more alert and sharpen their senses. No one should take large doses of vitamin D without the advice of a doctor. In megadoses it can cause bone problems and damage to the kidneys.

Students contend that vitamin B-12 counteracts the effects of drugs, both stimulants and depressants. Research does not bear this out.

In general, personality and mood changes may be due to thiamine deficiency; loss of control over arms and legs to B-12 deficiency; depression to folic-acid deficiency; and a feeling of "going crazy" to the advanced stages of niacin deficiency. Heavy dosages of vitamins should be used only under the direction of a physician. Should your child take vitamin supplements? If he or she isn't getting the vitamin RDA from food, the answer is yes. Nevertheless, the best source of vitamins is food. With a balanced diet, our children shouldn't require vitamin supplements.

To cope with what they perceive to be innumerable problems in their lives, along with other, undefined worries and tensions, countless children reach out for "remedies"—alcohol, junk food, cigarettes and marijuana, stimulants and depressants, and megavitamins. All of these substances are readily available, but while they may provide temporary relief from stress, they do not offer permanent solutions to students' problems. In most cases these substances not only delay an individual's ability to recognize the cause of distress, but also work against his or her ability to gain control of the problem.

TWELVE

SUICIDE

THE TRAGIC FACT IS THAT SUICIDE AMONG AMERI-
can students is escalating, according to the National Center for
Statistics. The World Health Organization has records of 1,000
suicides each day. After accidents, suicide is the leading cause of
death among college students.

- Students between the ages of fourteen and twenty-six comprise the highest suicide risk group, with nearly nineteen
  deaths per 100,000.
- The suicide rate for college students between seventeen
  and twenty-six years of age is 50 percent higher than for
  any other Americans in this age group.

These figures reflect actual suicides, not suicide attempts. The
number of attempts is nine times higher. In addition, there is
evidence that youngsters who attempt suicide once are four to
five times more likely to try it again. Also, youngsters with a
family history of suicide are more apt to attempt it.

Suicide is not an ordinary response to pressure, but it must be touched on in this book because the suicide rate among our children has been alarmingly high for over two decades, and informed parents may be able to spot their children responding abnormally under duress. Children might, of course, contemplate suicide in the face of overwhelming stress. They might dwell on the subject of suicide, consider what reactions their suicide would have on friends and family, and think about the various methods of suicide. Once again, this is *not* a normal reaction to stress. Children with healthy coping mechanisms *can* deal with the stressors of daily frustrations and even periodic tragedies.

Nevertheless, counselors are finding an increase of suicidal tendencies as a response to great stress. Children considering suicide usually send out a number of warning signals and display particular behavior patterns:

- persistent lack of motivation
- constant lethargy or lack of energy
- change in sleeping and/or eating habits
- decrease in sexual interest
- inability to concentrate
- difficulty in making decisions
- feelings of helplessness and hopelessness
- increased use/abuse of drugs

Not coincidentally, these same signals are symptoms of stress.

Although it is not uncommon for children to exhibit this kind of behavior from time to time, these symptoms are serious if they persist or if they occur in concert. If they do, parents must pay attention. Of course, the intensity of the signals differs from child to child.

Suicidal behavior results from feelings of depression, isolation, loneliness, despair, and the insecurity of not being able to solve an intolerable problem. The behavior of youngsters with suicidal tendencies stems from a desperate need to end an intolerable situation. This situation can be physical or psychological, mixed with feelings of ambivalence, confusion, or turmoil. The crux of the matter is that the child wants the problem to disappear, and suicide is regarded as a way of getting rid of the terrible dilemma. Needless to say, this is a totally inappropriate response to stress.

Among youngsters, depression, anxiety, and stress are characteristic symptoms in most suicide cases. In these instances, children seem to have lost

> a sense of belonging
> a sense of identity
> recognition from their peers
> a sense of self-esteem
> a sense of confidence
> assertiveness

Children tend to keep their thoughts of suicide to themselves. When a depressed youngster is incapable of finding a realistic solution to his or her problems, thinking becomes confused and only one alternative presents itself: If I destroy myself, then the problem is destroyed.

It has been found that suicide and alcoholism go hand in hand, although it is unclear whether the alcohol prevents the children from realizing they are actually going to kill themselves or merely removes inhibitions related to suicidal behavior. Even people who normally do not drink are inclined to take a drink shortly before killing themselves.

In most cases, it takes a combination of stresses to lead to self-destructive behavior. While an extreme incident can certainly trigger a student into taking his or her life, seldom is a single factor the cause of suicide. The rate of suicide attempts is somewhat determined by the degree of social integration. Children need to be part of a group—such as a family, peer group, or church or youth organization. The need to belong is inherent and helps the child cope by overcoming feelings of loneliness and isolation. Depression that results directly from loneliness or isolation can ultimately lead to suicide. For example, statistics show that most college student suicides occur early in the semester when many students leave family and friends behind for the school campus. This statistic confirms the need to belong, the significance of support groups and organizations.

The sense of loneliness of that first semester is heightened by the overcrowding that exists on so many campuses. This contributes to frustration and aggression and hinders a student's ability to concentrate on academic and personal goals. The other contributing factor is the computerized bureaucracy of many campuses, which largely ignores the student's need for personal contact. Many students become distressed at having to deal with computers and red tape. For these reasons, many campuses have created a Student Affairs division that acts as a counseling center for students. In the past year, the demand for such counseling services has tripled.

It is easy to understand why. Students often take courses in crowded classrooms in dilapidated buildings. The integration of interracial and foreign students on the campus requires a great deal of adjustment. Most students are under economic constraints. Finally, students are under great pressure to establish goals and achieve them. Today's college students don't feel they have the luxury of previous generations in exploring career opportunities, majors, or enjoying themselves. On the contrary, students now feel that because there are comparatively few desirable jobs available in the present economy, they don't have the leisure to evaluate academic choices and have a good time. They are too intent on pursuing goals, on acquiring the skills and knowledge necessary to get a decent job.

When a student grows angry and ultimately depressed with campus bureaucracy and depersonalization, he or she begins to internalize that anger or depression. This can mark a serious turning point. As students try to handle the mounting tension of excelling in school and finding a good job, they reach a breaking point. Some are unable to generate viable alternatives to their depression, to the tension of their lives. When they arrive at this breaking point and are unable to cope (or be "rescued" by outside help), suicide suggests itself as a possible alternative.

For students, depression results from persistent fluctuations in self-esteem or from a growing awareness of the difference between their idealism and society's materialism. Students' perception of their level of achievement often reflects their degree of self-esteem. Those performing below their capability don't necessarily become depressed, of course, but there is a fluctuation in self-esteem. Some will feel better about themselves when their performance improves, but not all students cope equally well with these fluctuations. If they can't cope, they feel painfully dejected.

There is no mistaking the fact that school is a pressurized environment, encompassing all of the following:

- passing all required courses
- fear of failing
- performance as a measure of self-esteem
- finding enough time to study and complete all class projects, themes, etc.
- fear of the unknown world of work after college
- the drive to succeed in a competitive environment
- social experiences, positive and negative
- the need to achieve goals

To this list must be added the personal liabilities of each student who has a role conflict or feels guilt for some personal reason.

Potential suicides tend to withdraw from others and into themselves as they attempt to figure out their problems. Unfortunately, this is self-defeating behavior in many cases; talking with friends or family is a healthier option and also provides the sense of belonging that is so essential to youngsters. Instead, the potential suicide keeps his or her own counsel, inviting a detrimental sense of alienation by withdrawal precisely at the time they should be seeking help from those who have significant meaning in their lives. As you might expect, the withdrawal period represents a very crucial time in a child's life. Another crucial period for the severely depressed child is when he or she is beginning to emerge from the depression. The child may at last be hopeful, but a sudden, drastic event can crush that hope. Parents should pay careful attention to children, especially during these two crucial periods.

For the most part, student suicide attempts can be divided into three categories:

1. **Children who have little intention of dying.** This category includes those who take drugs, take pills with alcohol, slash their wrists, crash their cars while drunk. This behavior is a cry for help, very often a nonverbal way of saying "I can't go on living this way" or "Something has got to change." The death may not be intended, it may occur during one of these desperate acts.

2. **Children who are ambivalent about dying.** The child is taking a gamble with his or her life, all the while hoping that someone will come to the rescue. A typical example is the student who threatens to take an overdose of sleeping pills if his girlfriend doesn't return his affection. If the girlfriend does not respond to the threat, the boy takes an overdose, placing a note in a prominent location so someone he likes will find it and rescue him. However, if the note isn't found in time, the boy might die.

3. **Children who attempt suicide but are rescued by luck.** Even though some children fully intend to kill themselves, most do not really want to, and are grateful if they are stopped in time. In fact, many children who are saved recover from their suicide attempts with a sense of elation. Many recover with a feeling of being reborn.

Since the incidence of suicide among students is rising, parents and teachers will need education and training in detection and prevention of suicide. The key element in being aware of the possibly suicidal child and offering assistance is concern. Most suicide signals can be picked up by anyone close to the child, but to genuinely help that child requires empathy.

What can we do to improve the emotional well-being of students who exhibit suicidal tendencies? The following guide should be effective.

1. **Help youngsters develop a sense of identity.**
   Children contend that it is hard to develop close, meaningful relationships in large and impersonal surroundings such as a school campus. Particularly large settings can be intimidating, especially if the child is accustomed to a smaller, more intimate environment.

2. **Help youngsters when you sense they are troubled.**
   It is important to be supportive the minute you suspect your child is having problems that he or she can't handle or isn't handling. Try to recognize what his or her needs are. The most significant help you can provide is the expression of concern, because that proves to the child that you care.

3. **Get help for youngsters if you suspect they are suicidal.**
   If you suspect that a child is suicidal, you should find professional help as soon as possible. At this juncture, there is no substitute for professional help.

The responsibility for helping suicidal children does not have to rest solely on parents and teachers. Communities can provide excellent assistance by establishing a suicide-prevention center staffed with people who know how to spot and help troubled children. These centers can intervene during a time of crisis to ameliorate its intensity. Staff members can become important to a child, for they are receptive and respect the principle of confidentiality as they work with the child. Dealing with the youngster's ambivalence is the single most important concept in suicide intervention, and staffs are certain to show the concern and empathy necessary to fight a child's ambivalence.

Since the impulse to commit suicide is fleeting, suicide-prevention centers provide an effective avenue for helping troubled children. Students are inclined to be self-destructive for only relatively short periods of time, and thus allow staff members to guide them through these periods.

There is no question that parents and teachers need to be alert to evidence of suicidal behavior. About 75 percent of suicidal students leave clues that indicate they are thinking about suicide. Basically, there are three kinds of clues:

1. **Situational.**
   The child's situation is conducive to thinking about and planning suicide.
2. **Syndromatic.**
   The child exhibits various symptoms associated with the syndrome of depression, which is the syndrome usually associated with a suicidal state of mind.
3. **Verbal.**
   The child expresses his or her preoccupation with suicide. Some verbal clues are clear messages of a wish to die, such as, "I can't take it any longer," "No one needs me anymore."

It is extremely difficult to be certain that a troubled child will or will not commit suicide. There is no handy personality profile available for a parent to consult as to the probability of a particular child committing suicide. For the time being, the best indicator scale of a potential suicide is the one devised by the Los Angeles Suicide Prevention Center. To assess the probability that a student might carry out a suicide threat, the center relies on this index:

1. **Age and Sex.**
   The probability is greater if the child is male rather than female, and for boys between the ages of fifteen and twenty-five and girls between ten and sixteen.
2. **Symptoms.**
   The probability is greater if the child manifests such symptoms as sleep disturbances, depression, feelings of hopelessness or isolation, a sense of powerlessness, or alcoholism.

3. **Stress.**
   The probability is greater if the child is experiencing stress from the loss of a parent because of death or divorce, from increased responsibilities, from serious illness, or other major stressors.

4. **Acute vs. Chronic Aspects.**
   The immediate probability is greater if there is a sudden onslaught of specific symptoms. The long-term probability is greater if there is a recurrence of specific symptoms or a recent increase in long-standing maladaptive behavior.

5. **Suicidal Plan.**
   The probability is greater in proportion to the lethal nature of the suicide method and the child's clarity about the plan.

6. **Resources.**
   The probability is greater if the child has no family or friends, or if family and friends are unwilling to help.

7. **Prior Suicidal Behavior.**
   The probability is greater if the child has a history of prior attempts or a history of repeated threats and depression.

8. **Medical Status.**
   The probability is greater if the child suffers from a chronic, debilitating illness or has had many unsuccessful experiences with physicians.

9. **Communication Aspects.**
   The probability is greater if the child has no communication with family or friends or if the child rejects efforts of family and friends to communicate with him or her.

10. **Reaction of Important Friends.**
    The probability is greater if friends or family whom the child considers important reject him or her and deny that the child needs help.

The greatest danger for all parents regarding teen suicide is the belief that "My child would never do that." Most parents of teenagers who have successfully or unsuccessfully attempted suicide are initially surprised that their children have moved in this direction, but on closer analysis realize that there were warning signs that they ignored, unaware of their significance.

PART V

WAYS TO COPE WITH STRESS IN CHILDREN

THIRTEEN

STRESS-MANAGEMENT PROGRAMS FOR CHILDREN

PROGRAMS OR ENRICHING EXPERIENCES SPECIFI-
cally designed to give youngsters opportunities to develop sophisticated skills in managing stress are as yet relatively scarce.
Fortunately, however, there are a few exemplary models.

Quieting Reflex

"Magic Breathing Hole" in Monessen, Pennsylvania, is one such
program. It is designed to help children discriminate between
positive and negative bodily sensations and to understand their
own abilities to adjust physiological responses to stressful situations. Short exercises are based on a relaxation concept called
QR (quieting reflex). It is used in classrooms of healthy children
and also in treating children who suffer from stress-related symptoms such as migraine headaches, high blood pressure, and stomach disturbances. The object of QR is to reverse the internal
changes that occur when a child reacts to a situation with fear

or alarm. In short, QR helps children express and deal with their feelings in an acceptable way.

QR, described as a "mini-tranquilizer," was developed by Dr. Charles Stroebel to combat the body's response to stress. It is a six-second technique of calming the body when the natural response is to run away from a situation or to attack aggressively. In many instances these responses are neither appropriate nor acceptable. The whole point of QR is to reverse these natural reactions by

1. becoming aware of what is bothering you;
2. consciously relaxing facial muscles and even smiling in order to remain calm;
3. taking a long, deep breath, then exhaling slowly, letting your jaw go limp.

QR has a distinct advantage as a stress-management tool in that it is done on the spot for ony six seconds. Furthermore, this technique for handling stress can be used effectively to counteract the current medical practice of prescribing tranquilizers as a quick therapy for stress-related disorders.

QR is often adapted into exercises that invoke imaginary friends to help youngsters deal with real feelings. QR exercises help youngsters automatically adjust their bodies to meet the immediate stress. While youngsters have less control over their environment than adults, they are more capable of modifying their responses in shorter periods of time. It has been found that adults can learn QR in four to six months, whereas children are able to master these relaxation skills with ease in two to three weeks.

High levels of arousal, if frequent or prolonged, can result in muscle tension, headaches, elevated blood pressure and cholesterol levels, and upset stomachs. The goal—as in biofeedback—is to change the physiological reaction to stress.

In classrooms like the one in Pennsylvania, children are learning the same QR technique that has been tested on thousands of adults with biofeedback. The program, called "Kiddie QR," does not require expensive biofeedback equipment or specially trained teachers. Youngsters are able to distinguish quickly between situations that require action (such as catching a bus) and those that require a different kind of behavior (the calm and alertness needed in preparation for taking a test). Nearly 600 school districts across the country are using Kiddie QR regularly in the classroom. Researchers are now applying Kiddie QR to atypical children, too—cerebral-palsy patients, the gifted, the hyperactive, and the abused.

Other Programs

Another program, headed by faculty members at UCLA, is offered by the Center for Health Enhancement. Dr. Jonathan Fielding contends that there is overwhelming evidence of the necessity for and ability of people to take responsibility for their health and wellness. One of the most striking features of the program is a twenty-four-day period in which individuals try to achieve lasting wellness through learning about the relationship of life-style to well-being.

In 1979 Dr. Christopher Wilson of the San Diego County Department of Education proposed a project in which students in grades seven, eight, and nine would be taught self-control and stress-management techniques. The program has produced some remarkable results. For instance, teachers and administrators from many of the twenty pilot schools reported noticeable grade improvements among students directly involved with the program or whose teachers had completed the training.

Research has given rise to the belief that youngsters can be taught to control their autonomic reactions (heart rate, breathing, muscle tension) via such techniques as biofeedback training, visualization, and meditation. The work of various researchers suggests that stress levels can be controlled through body awareness, and that improved stress levels result in improvement of other behavior. For this reason, model programs such as Project P.R.E.S. (Physical Response Education System) offered through the Santa Cruz County Office of Education are providing new insight.

Acupressure

The results of an initial informal investigation by Santa Cruz, in which acupressure training was used as a means of physical-response education for severely handicapped children, suggest that this new technique may have remarkable potential in effecting physical, social/emotional, cognitive, communicative, and health breakthroughs and growth for youngsters.

Essentially, acupressure is a form of directed therapeutic touch that does not involve the use of needles. In an acupressure session, there is continuous one-to-one physical contact. The person delivering the acupressure uses hands and fingers to stimulate the points where an acupuncturist would insert needles and holds these points until there is a body response that indicates a release of tension. This slow-paced touch (usually one to three minutes at each pair of points along the body) evokes the experience of being held, cradled, safe. It is a highly intimate, supportive interaction between the two people involved.

This method has been particularly beneficial to developmentally delayed children since a major obstacle in educating such youngsters has been the lack of educational tools that would enable the teacher, aides, and parents actually to reach children at their most basic level of psychophysical functioning.

The efficacy of acupressure is based on the rationale supported by research that body-awareness techniques effectively relieve stress, and that any level of learning, from the most basic to the most sophisticated, is more likely to occur when the learner is not under duress. Both educational and medical research have validated the concept that a relaxed but attentive mind and body are essential conditions in the learning process.

Yoga and Meditation Philosophies

Yoga and other meditation philosophies have been recognized for thousands of years for their ability to quiet the mind, steady the emotions, slow respiration, make muscles supple, regulate internal organs, reduce heart rate and blood pressure, and produce mental and muscular rest and renewal. These techniques, however, often require extensive training in mental and physical exercises to achieve relaxation and mental efficiency.

Biofeedback

Biofeedback is a process by which electronic equipment is used to relay physiological information to the individual. Biofeedback is simply the feedback of internal, ongoing biological states. A thermometer, for example, is a biofeedback instrument because it feeds back information on body temperature. More recently, thermometers have been updated and now there is an electronic thermometer that is used as a biofeedback tool.

Other electronic machines have been developed to provide us with information about our bodily states. Perhaps the most well known is the electroencephalograph (EEG), which reports the amount of electrical activity occurring in the brain. Another widely known tool is the electrocardiograph (EKG), which reports the electrical activity of the heart as it pumps. Similarly, the amount of electrical activity in the muscles is reported by the electromyograph, and electrical temperature machines provide information on body temperature from spots other than the mouth.

Research conducted over the last twenty-five years has shown that many internal functions, such as blood pressure and body temperature, can be consciously controlled, and that individuals can be taught how to do it. Control is achieved by interacting with the machine that provides the information and experiencing how a specific function, such as blood pressure, is influenced by various thoughts, feelings, or moods. Children seem to thoroughly enjoy working with these machines, and repeated sessions result in learning how to control various functions, but not everyone learns equally well. By showing individuals how to control the tenseness of the muscle located across the temple through EMG training, we can teach them how to be more relaxed and calm. By listening to the machine—which provides an electronic click for a specified level of tenseness—or watching a digital display—which reflects numerically the amount of tension being experienced—individuals can learn how to reduce the tension and how to relax.

The implications of biofeedback are far-reaching: A child can voluntarily control involuntary processes such as muscle tension, skin temperature, blood pressure, heartbeat, and even certain brain-wave patterns—which in turn provides treatment of certain psychosomatic illness processes. The long-term effects are significant, since the child learns self-control over a variety of emotional and physical states.

Dynamic Psychotherapy

This intervention technique reduces and frequently eliminates the stress response by providing information or insights about the stressor, and/or about the youngster's reason for perceiving something as a stressor or threat. A skilled therapist can help youngsters mobilize the subconscious and help fears surface to conscious awareness so that they can be dealt with.

Hypnotherapy

Hypnotherapy is an effective technique for resolving difficulties in adjusting to stress, tension, and anxiety.

All methods of hypnotherapy involve the use of one or another hypnotic technique, such as hypeamnesia or posthypnotic suggestions. A sampling of the scope of therapeutic applications includes migraines, muscular rheumatism, insomnia, asthma, multiple sclerosis, epilepsy, and seasickness.

Youngsters are helped to cope with stress by utilizing the peaceful state of mind that can be achieved under hypnosis. This form of relaxation enables the thought processes to slow down and become more orderly. Often this tranquillity restores confidence as anxieties, doubts, and fears dissipate. Perhaps one of the greatest effects of hypnotherapy is that the serenity of the mind continues after wakening and becomes more prolonged with repeated inductions and sessions. Students can learn to enter the hypnotic state of temporarily altered consciousness by properly instructed and qualified psychological practitioners.

All these techniques have proved helpful in stress management, so if any of them interest you and you have the opportunity to pursue them, by all means do so. If not, the following chapter provides numerous stress-management skills that any parent and child can practice.

FOURTEEN

REDUCING STRESS BY ALLEVIATING ITS SYMPTOMS

When a youngster is troubled by a specific symptom associated with a variety of stressors, symptom-directed intervention is appropriate, especially when the youngster cannot tell what is bothering him—he knows only that he is upset. In cases where it is not possible to eliminate the causes of stress, it becomes necessary to attack the symptoms.

Some of the more common symptoms treated with symptom-directed intervention include tension headaches, hypertension, chest pain, stomach pain, low back pain, fatigue, overeating, depression, lethargy, and others listed below. Displaced tension can result in any number of physical symptoms.

cold, clammy, or clenched hands

constipation or diarrhea

continual desire to cry (or crying)

inability to sleep or nightmares

increased appetite or loss of appetite (overeating or not eating)

coughing
depression
dry mouth or throat
excessive snacking
fatigue
fear, panic, or anxiety
finger-tapping, foot-tapping, pencil-tapping
frigidity
frowning
grinding teeth
headache, dizziness
hives

nausea or stomach pains
nervous tic
pacing
rash or acne
restlessness
stuttering
increased smoking or chain-smoking
increased perspiring
irritability or bad temper
lethargy or inability to work
level of blood pressure
loss of sex drive
low-grade infections
muscular aches

An invaluable parental goal would be to help youngsters learn to recognize their own signs of stress. These signs are evidence that tension has been unconsciously shifted from the overt source of stress to the body, and we must teach children how to heed the warnings the body is sending out. An argument with a friend, for example, can be "translated" into a physical symptom such as a stomachache, headache, or backache. Even worse is that this displacing process can become a habit, building and maintaining chronic tension over a period of time. We hear about the youngster who is always "uptight" or "high-strung." Over a period of time, the original source of the tension becomes buried and the *response habit* is formed. Therefore, it sometimes becomes necessary to eliminate the physical symptom in order to define the problem.

The importance of teaching youngsters systematic approaches and techniques in health management cannot be overemphasized. Taking time to relax, for example, is an important step toward the prevention of stress disorders. There are a variety of techniques to lower the stress-response threshold. The purpose of this chapter is to explore some of these techniques and provide ways to help youngsters apply them in their own lives.

Relaxation Techniques

Relaxation techniques have been acknowledged as a useful elixir in curing many problems and illnesses, such as migraine and tension headaches, peptic ulcers, insomnia, nail-biting, acute dermatitis, asthma, stuttering, depression, anxiety, and hypertension. Some researchers and clinicians would add alcoholism and drug abuse to this list.

It is only in the last decade that we have become aware of the tremendous potential for physical self-regulation, and, better yet, the potential for optimal health and prevention of disease. Human beings have a remarkable capacity to affect and control their physiologies and nervous systems. This process is unconscious, however, and children tend not to realize their own potential for influencing their bodies.

We have begun to realize the extent to which self-healing and self-regulation of bodily processes are possible. After we have become aware of physiological functioning and physical responses to stress, we can then appropriately apply coping techniques, which can be used to accomplish both of these goals for our children. With practice, relaxation can become a more automatic response to stress than tension.

Earlier we noted that a physical response to stress can become a habit. While being aware of the cause of a specific stressor is the first step, something else must be done. A technique is needed to remedy the condition. Relaxation is one such method. Relaxation can be used to unlearn physical responses that have become habits and to eradicate the physical symptoms of chronic tension, especially if it has been allowed to accumulate over the years.

Relaxation is also useful in coping with situations that are unlikely to change. An incredible amount of energy can be wasted in trying to change a situation that simply cannot be changed.

Such useless efforts are likely to increase rather than decrease stress levels.

Teaching youngsters relaxation techniques helps them slow down. Many youngsters operate at a high level of activity that can be pointless, nondirective, and nonproductive. Such an increase in activity level serves only to disorganize a youngster, and as the child becomes more behaviorally disorganized, he is likely to come into conflict with the people around him, particularly peers, parents, and teachers. Relaxation can be a way of rechanneling some of that excess energy. It can also be a way to help focus attention and to learn concentration. This is helpful since distractability is a primary problem for many youngsters, some of whom are unable to focus effectively on one thing for very long. If they can be given techniques like relaxation to help them focus more effectively, they may overcome this problem. Being able to pay attention can lead to improved memory and certainly increases a child's capacity to learn.

Relaxation is healthy. Relaxing is a natural and needed activity for our bodies. When we become tense or overactive, we must relax in order to bring our biological systems into balance. People who go for a long time at a chronically high level of tension may experience physical and emotional problems. Youngsters in particular miss out on important learning by being unable to focus on any one thing for a sufficient period of time.

Relaxation helps us "self-balance" and thus stay physically healthy. Youngsters tend to be very reactive—that is, they will often respond to situations without thinking. There are numerous situations at school and at home where impulsive reacting can cause major problems. For example, a child may record the first answer that comes to mind on a test, regardless of whether or not it is correct; or grab the first puzzle piece within reach and try to fit it in without considering the puzzle as a whole. After a few such tries, the child may become very frustrated with this process and give up trying, perhaps feeling that he has failed. A cycle of failures like this does nothing to increase the child's self-esteem; it only increases his frustration.

Social and interpersonal situations can also suffer from reacting without thinking first. If one child bumps into another accidentally, the second child may respond by hitting, which usually leads to trouble. If, however, the child can learn to slow down and think before responding, this can be avoided. Just stopping and then slowing down gives the child an opportunity to assess a situation before reacting impulsively. Rechanneling the excess energy by relaxing also decreases the potential for impulsive behavior. Thus, relaxation can be seen as one way to help children gain self-control. It has been found that when children feel this sense of self-control or self-mastery, their self-confidence goes up, too. Certainly, being able to increase their success at completing a task, like the puzzle, makes a huge difference to children who are frustrated from repeated failures.

Diaphragmatic Breathing

Controlling one's breathing, or breathing in a special way for a few minutes, is often an effective way to relax. Breathing exercises are commonly used in yoga and meditation. Breathing that involves a long, slow exhalation is relaxing. When you take in air, your diaphragm expands and tenses. As you let the air out, or exhale, it relaxes. So one way to relax is to lengthen the time you spend exhaling. Diaphragmatic breathing not only encourages you to use your full capacity for breathing, filling the lungs entirely with air, but also emphasizes a long, slow exhalation, thus relaxing.

Many yoga experts assert that most people do not know how to breathe properly, often using the chest in short, shallow breaths. This type of breathing—thoracic breathing—is inappropriate and is thought to be indicative of unrecognized tension. It may also be detrimental to health since stale and unused air is retained in the lungs. The proper, healthy way to breathe is diaphragmatic, or "belly breathing," the way babies and animals breathe.

As fresh air is inhaled, the bloodstream is oxygenated and purified. In addition, breathing has a major impact on heart function. Breathing slowly and regularly while sitting upright causes the heart rate to decelerate. Conversely, shallow and quick breathing while slouching accelerates the heart. Yogic breathing, deep breathing, or diaphragmatic breathing counteracts the tension-producing pattern of shallow breathing. When breathing deeply, the rate of respiration is automatically slowed down. With practice, a rate of fifteen to twenty breaths per minute can be decreased to only five or six.

The following exercise is designed to help you teach youngsters how to relax. It can be used almost anytime or anywhere. Follow these steps:

1. Get comfortable. Move your arms and legs around to make your muscles loose.
2. Close your eyes.
3. Take a deep breath *in* and count slowly: one ... two ... three ... four.
4. Let the air out very slowly, counting one ... two ... three ... four ... five ... six.
5. Repeat the above, but this time place your hands on your stomach and feel it filling up with air (pushing out) when you breathe.
6. Breathe in deeply: one ... two ... three ... four.
7. Let the air out slowly: one ... two ... three ... four ... five ... six (feel your stomach pull back in).
8. Repeat this a few more times.
9. Open your eyes.
10. Now how do you feel?

In order to give youngsters adequate practice in using this breathing pattern, a three-to-five-minute "time-out" session each day is recommended. The breathing technique can be used alone or in combination with other relaxation exercises such as progressive muscle relaxation or visualization.

Progressive Muscle Relaxation

Progressive muscle relaxation is a technique that creates awareness of tension and relaxation and teaches a way to relax all the muscles. It is called "progressive" because it proceeds through all of the major muscle groups, relaxing them one at a time until eventually there's total muscle relaxation.

Progressive muscle relaxation can be used to relax completely or to relax only certain muscles. For example, people who work at a desk several hours a day find it helpful to do a neck or shoulder exercise to loosen up those muscles. The technique also helps one become aware of when a single muscle starts to tighten up. Many times people become tense without knowing it, until they have a headache, backache, or neckache. By becoming more keenly aware of when and where the tension starts, many conditions, such as headaches, can be totally avoided. It is much better to relax a neck muscle for a few minutes than to lie down to recover from a painful headache.

Muscle relaxation is not only an important relaxation tool for children, it also facilitates body awareness. This can be extremely useful in helping overactive children, too. If they can become aware of their own arousal levels and identify them as such, and then apply a relaxation technique to decrease those levels, they can exert much more control over their behavior.

Progressive relaxation involves selectively tensing and relaxing various muscles and noting causative sensations. Very often, youngsters are simply not aware of the amount of muscle tension they are experiencing, nor of what relaxation actually feels like.

To teach your child progressive muscle relaxation, have him tense a muscle, then relax it. He will notice the contrast between the feeling of tension in a muscle and the feeling of relaxation of that muscle. Have your child inhale as he tenses a muscle, then exhale as he relaxes it. Spend more time relaxing than tensing. Eventually, the tensing effort can be dropped. To learn this technique, begin with the following exercise:

1. Fists: Clench right fist, then left, then both.
2. Biceps: Bend elbows, tense biceps.
3. Triceps: Straighten and feel tension along back of arms.
4. Forehead: Wrinkle forehead, frown.
5. Eyes: Squint, then close tightly.

6. Jaws: Clench jaw, grind teeth together.
7. Tongue: Press against roof of mouth.
8. Lips: Press together.
9. Neck: Press your head back as far as it will go; roll to right, roll to left, bring head forward to chest.
10. Shoulders: Shrug one, then the other, and then both.
11. Chest: Fill lungs with air, hold, and breathe out.
12. Stomach: Tighten stomach muscles; push stomach out.
13. Lower back: Arch up back, make lower back hollow, feel tension along spine.
14. Buttocks and Thighs: Flex by pressing down on heels; then straighten knees and flex again.
15. Calves: Press feet and toes downward, tensing calf muscles.
16. Ankles and Shins: Bend feet toward head, feeling tension along shins.

Often when we are nervous, our muscles get tense or tight. This next exercise will teach you to feel the difference between tense and relaxed muscles, and help you learn to relax all of your muscles. For this exercise, close your eyes and relax while the instructions are read to you.

1. Get comfortable, either lying down or sitting in a chair. Your legs should be uncrossed and straight out in front of you. Let your arms rest at your sides.
2. Take a deep breath and let the air out slowly.
3. Make a fist with your right hand and tighten the muscles. Then let it go, relax it. Do the same with your other hand. Then make a fist with both hands at the same time. Then relax them.
4. Now tighten your whole area; stretch both arms out, away from your body. Then relax; let them flop back down at your sides. Do this a couple of times.
5. Shrug your shoulders up high, toward your ears. Then let them drop back down and relax. Do this twice, too.
6. Bend your head first to one side, then to the other.

Feel the muscles tighten on one side of your neck as they relax on the other.

7. Roll your head around in a circle, slowly. Feel your neck muscles loosen up.

8. Press your lips together. Then loosen them.

9. This time open your mouth wide—like a lion roaring—and also feel your jaw muscles stretching. Then relax them when you close your mouth.

10. Now fill your lungs with air. Breathe in, hold your breath for a few seconds, then breathe out.

11. Pull your stomach in. Make it hard and feel your stomach muscles tighten. Now let go and let them relax.

12. Arch your back, making it hollow behind you. Then relax.

13. Now tighten your leg muscles. First point your toes away from you. Stretch your legs out away from you. Feel the tension in your leg muscles. Then stop pointing and let them relax. Second, bend your feet back at the ankles. Point your toes toward your head. Feel the tight muscles. Now let them relax. Let your feet relax and your legs relax.

14. Take a few more deep breaths, without tensing your muscles. Relax for a few moments. How do your muscles feel now? How do you feel?

15. Sit up slowly. Take another deep breath and stretch your arms, just like you do when you wake up in the morning.

It is important to include a termination process at the end of each relaxation exercise. This process consists of flexing the arms, taking a deep breath, and slowly opening the eyes. This helps the system adjust gradually to the higher state of arousal needed for getting up and walking around.

You might say, "I'm going to count from four to one. When I reach one, your eyes will open and you will be awake, feeling calm and comfortable. OK, four... three... two... one, eyes open, feeling calm and comfortable." The count is done slowly, allowing the relaxation period to be ended easily and quietly. Since it is similar to a sleep state, the termination steps allow a better transition to the alert phase.

Note to parents: Use relaxation techniques at least once a week with your child. Make a point of doing this by allowing your child to observe *you* taking time out to relax, talking yourself through it, and describing how you feel afterward: "That feels much better. Now I feel calm."

Autogenic Training

Another relaxation technique is that of autogenic training. The word *autogenic* means self-generating. Autogenic training is a therapeutic approach that trains the child to exercise control over his physiology. The goal is to teach the child certain self-normalizing, recuperative processes that are directed and coordinated by the brain. It assumes that our own biological system best knows what adaptions it needs to make in order to function at an optimal level of health. This method involves using mental and bodily functions simultaneously to achieve homeostasis, or "self-balancing." Concentration on a verbal autogenic formula is maintained during practice. The content, or the formula, and the sequence of the different exercises are designed to adapt to the particular disorders that the individual is experiencing. Autogenic methods can best be adopted for the treatment of psychosomatic behavior and vasomotor disturbances.

The benefits from autogenic training generally include an increase in emotional and physiological tolerance, less inhibited and more natural social interactions, increased objectivity, and enhanced overall capacity to cope.

Visualization and Imagery

Imagery and visualization are frequently used in holistic medicine for self-healing. Only recently has imagination been used purposely for self-healing in our Western culture. However, the impact of thought processes upon physiological functioning has long been recognized in other cultures.

Visualization is a powerful tool in relaxation. It can be an induced and deliberate process. Utilization of imagery for relaxation purposes usually involves creating a pleasurable scene in the mind—one that is associated with relaxation. Youngsters are instructed to develop a scene in their minds and picture themselves in it. They are verbally encouraged to relax. Some youngsters may have difficulty beginning the visualization process on their own, so a technique called "guided imagery" is used. The purpose is to provide a series of images to stimulate visualization and specifically direct the development of a desired scene (examples are provided below).

To become proficient at visualization, it is helpful to begin with exercises proceeding from simple to more complex images, using the steps outlined below. Each step is a plateau in learning visualization. Once children are able to visualize freely, they can create and direct their own scenes.

1. Get comfortable and close your eyes.
2. Relax your muscles. You may use breathing, muscle-relaxation, or autogenic exercises to become relaxed.
3. Imagine or picture yourself doing something relaxing. Get the full picture in your mind.
4. Continue relaxing for a few minutes, picturing yourself in a relaxing scene.
5. When you are finished, stretch your arms, take a deep breath, and open your eyes.

Ideas for Visualizations for Children

- It is a lazy Saturday morning. Everyone is still asleep. A gentle rain is falling outside. You are still sleepy. The house is cool. You pull the warm covers up around you and snuggle back into your warm bed....
- Tomorrow is your birthday. You listen to everyone busily planning surprises for you. You are supposed to stay in your room while they prepare surprises for you. You feel warmed by the love, attention, and planning that is going on for you....

• You are sitting in the warm sun. It makes you feel nice and warm and comfortable, even sort of sleepy. You stretch out and lie in the sun. You can hear birds in the trees around you, see the gentle blue sky, and hear the quiet hum of automobiles far away. You have all of your activities done, and the feelings of laziness are so good. . . .

Your Own Visualization

It's wise to practice the visualization exercise and to create some ideas of your own. Look at the following questions. Using your imagination, create your own relaxing picture.

1. Name a place that makes you feel relaxed. _____
   _____

2. Put yourself in a beautiful setting. What are you doing? _____
   _____

3. What's the weather like there? _____
   _____

4. How do you feel when you are there? _____
   _____

5. Why would you like to return? _____
   _____

Now that you have your own visualization picture, you can practice relaxing with it. You might also want to share your ideas with others.

The Management of Behavior

How to help youngsters manage behavior (commonly referred to as behavior modification) can be of serious concern for parents. Occasionally, parents will need to help children understand and use behavioral interventions—techniques to help them assume responsibility for their actions. Teaching youngsters behavioral techniques leads to the improvement of self-control and enhances self-esteem. The ultimate goal is to help youngsters develop strategies so they can interrupt and alter their own behavior and thereby become more self-controlling.

Reinforcing Behavior

When youngsters demonstrate positive behavior, it must be reinforced with a positive response. These suggestions will be useful:

- Reinforce immediately after a positive behavior is displayed.
- In the early stages of learning a new behavior, reinforce every correct response. As behavior becomes stronger, require more correct responses before reinforcing.
- Never reinforce the wrong behavior.

For Parents and Youngsters

Try the following exercise:

1. Describe the behavior you would like your (child/parent) to change.

   _____

   _____

2. If this behavior is to be decreased, what behavior is to be increased, or reinforced?_____

   _____

3. What type of reinforcement are you going to use (praise, rewards, awards, etc.)?_____

   _____

Now see how you fare:

Child's/parent's behavior.	What reinforcement was used? (What was said or done?)	What was the result of using this reinforcement?
1.		
2.		
3.		
4.		

Using Your Newly Acquired Skills

The next phase is to use the techniques described in this chapter to make a personal plan for coping with stress. The goal is to keep using what you have learned.

What Did I Learn?

Please write your answers to the following questions in the space provided. This will help you remember the important points.

1. What is stress? _____

_____

2. Where does it come from? (Give two examples.)
   (a.) _____
   (b.) _____
3. How can stress affect your feelings? _____

_____

4. How can stress affect you physically? _____

_____

5. Name one way to cope with stress. _____

_____

   Now that you have reviewed and acquired stress-management skills, you must incorporate them into your life-style if they are to change your behavior effectively. The degree of behavioral change will depend on how much effort you invest in the process.

   Keeping weekly track of stress and the effectiveness of the coping techniques you use is an excellent way to sharpen your skills in managing stress, changing an undesired behavior, and maintaining a desired one. The following work sheet should help.

MY PLAN FOR COPING WITH STRESS

Area(s) I want to work on: _____

_____

_____

I will do this by (How will you do it?): _____

_____

_____

I will do this (How often?): _____

_____

I am doing this so that: _____

_____

_____

_____

(Sign your name)

_____

(Date)

A CONTRACT WITH MYSELF

I, _____, am making a commitment to myself to change
the following behavior: _____

_____

_____

I will do this by (technique and date/time) _____

_____

_____

I will do this (how often) _____

_____

I am doing this so that_____

_____

_____

I will reward myself by feeling good about myself and_____

_____

_____

_____

(Signature)

Completed_____   Not completed_____

I rewarded myself   Reasons_____

Yes_____No_____   _____

_____

_____

Be honest with yourself and you'll find the rewards coming as
you reduce the stress in your life and feel better about yourself.

FIFTEEN

TEACHING CHILDREN TECHNIQUES FOR STRESS PREVENTION

We are taught many things about health, but rarely how to prevent tension, much less reduce anxiety and stress. Yet the ability to manage stress successfully is especially necessary in children's lives since so much of their existence involves continual change, clarification of values, and forced choices. Unexpected or unfamiliar situations requiring unfamiliar coping skills produce a great deal of stress for our children. Those children who learn self-awareness and effective methods for managing the stresses that are sure to occur in everyday life are likely to be healthy, happy, and have a zest and zeal for living. By learning the goals and principles of coping, youngsters can draw vitality from stress and use it constructively to promote health fitness and self-development.

We can better enable our children to have productive and enjoyable lives during their formative years *by helping them to more adequately perceive their own resources.* If youngsters are to live a more stress-free life, they will need to develop efficient and effective skills in problem-solving, in generating acceptable alternatives to dilemmas, and in coping with accelerated change that is sure to be a part of their lives. These skills are vital if they are to gain a true and purposeful understanding of the world.

How our children will deal with stress during their adult years is determined to a great extent by what happens during their formative, impressionable years. Many scientific studies have proved how important early experiences are in influencing later behavior. This is another reason that parents should make every effort to help youngsters develop effective techniques in managing stress. To do so, parents must evaluate their youngsters' capabilities, set reasonable expectations for achievement, and seek to provide youngsters with an opportunity to gain emotional security.

Managing and reducing stress require hard work from both parents and children. Parents must help their children develop their resources, teaching them to focus on their own well-being and uniqueness as a means for successfully adjusting to their surroundings and to society as a whole. Stress management emphasizes enhancement of health and well-being through therapeutic and preventive care, and physical and emotional fitness.

Awareness

Maintaining good health requires effort and responsibility.

The channel through which people experience their being is awareness. It is both the ground floor of existence and a multilevel process through which we achieve the highest levels of self-actualization. To have awareness is to know what you are really seeing, hearing, thinking, feeling, saying, and doing. When people are fundamentally aware, they have all their inner and outer channels or receptors open. Aware people are fully receptive to their inner and outer environments and are therefore prepared and equipped to function responsively and responsibly in relation to themselves and others.

Youngsters must have a good understanding and awareness of stress and stressors as well as the skills and techniques for managing them. This is crucial if youngsters are to accept and have a commitment to their responsibility for generating commonsense approaches to the debilitating effects of stress. These commonsense approaches provide a sound basis for gaining and keeping a high level of wellness and for emphasizing the importance of low-stress living in maintaining good health.

Among episodic bouts of exhilaration and disappointment in the rush of daily living, youngsters often overlook the basic importance of rest, diet, nutrition, moderation, and positive habits that contribute to emotional and physical well-being. These factors are vital because they enhance health and can ease the impact of stressors within a youngster's environment. Even more important, sustaining good health in adulthood is often dependent on good health maintenance in those early years.

The following work sheets will help you guide youngsters to an understanding of what stress is, how it affects the body and mind, and what their role is in reducing and controlling the stressors they encounter.

Discuss these statements with your child, completing the list.

WHAT CAUSES STRESS?

Stress can result from what happens between people, such as:

1. When your parents are angry at you;

2. When you are tired of waiting in a long line; or

3. _____

OR

You can cause your own stress, such as:

1. When you think you are not smart enough;

2. When you feel you are not attractive enough; or

3. _____

WHAT DOES STRESS DO TO YOU?

Stress can affect you *physically*. For example:
- Your heart beats faster.
- Your hands get cold or sweaty.
- Your muscles get tight.
- Your stomach hurts.

Stress can affect your *emotions*. For example:
- You get nervous.
- You might feel sad, or giggle a lot.
- You might cry or want to hit out or strike out at something.
- You might daydream or dream a lot at night about something fearful.

Stress can also affect your *behavior*. For instance:
- You might be grouchy toward others.
- You can't concentrate in school.
- You might be more irritable or sarcastic with friends.

The Stress Cycle

When events in our lives get out of hand, what happens in one situation can lead to what will happen in another. The cycle of stress that results manifests itself in symptoms, and ultimately results in impaired functioning—in relations with others or in physical and/or emotional well-being. Any number or types of events—referred to as "demands" or "stressors"—can begin a cycle of stress. The effect of the stressor will depend upon the youngster's ability to deal adequately or cope with it. For this reason you'll want to teach your youngster to gain an adequate awareness and understanding of how stress evolves and is manifested psychologically, physiologically, and behaviorally. Ultimately, you want to teach your child to exercise control—to stop and think before reacting to different situations. You can begin this process by using the stress cycle pictured in figure 1 and the questions that follow.

FIG. 1
THE STRESS CYCLE

10. Next...

1. Your *best* friend sits with someone else on the bus this morning, and doesn't pay attention to you! It doesn't feel good.

9. Your sister teases you about staying after school, and you respond by hitting her. That makes you feel even worse.

2. To top it off, when you get to school, you can't remember your locker combination; this makes you late for class, and you can't hand your assignment in on time. You are really disgusted, because you worked so hard to complete it.

8. You had been planning on that game all week. Now that you can't go, you are really MAD!

3. Your teacher says she won't allow you to go to the office to get help on opening your locker, and won't accept the assignment because now it is late.

7. Because you stayed after school, you couldn't attend the San Diego Chargers football game with your father. You had really been looking forward to this.

4. Now that you have received a failing grade on the assignment you worked so hard on, you refuse to take the new assignment due tomorrow.

6. You shout back, "Stupid yourself!" but the teacher catches only you. Now you have to stay after school for 30 minutes.

5. You kick the desk that you bumped into on your way back to your seat. The student in it responds by saying, "Watch out, stupid."

Questions for Children

Of course, you could write your own script. But did you notice in the example how one event seemed to lead to another, which in turn affected the response in the next circumstance?

Notice what happens to you when an unpleasant event occurs and you aren't able to get in charge or stop other events from following. Do you see, as in the example, that each event influences and often provokes the next one?

What Can You Do?

You can decide to concentrate, to cope with these situations in a healthy and productive manner, or you can decide that you are out of control and will allow whatever happens to just sort of happen. People can work together to reduce the stress they are likely to encounter. An important lesson to learn from the stress cycle is that when you become overstressed, a likely response is anger; this makes it easy to yell at others or blame them for your problem. You unload or dump your feelings on someone, and this is unfair.

You can learn to make good stress work for you—like really concentrating when you know you must get back in control. You can learn to reduce the "bad" stress in your life. When stress gets to be a problem, we need to learn ways to cope with it, or ways to break the stress cycle. Design your own tool for coping with stress. Use the next example to look at your own real-life situation.

For Parent and Youngster

How do you respond? Together, see if you can re-create an instance when one event greatly affected the next, and led to stress. Make your own stress cycle.

                    9   1

            8   2

        7   3

            6   4

                5

Developing Support Systems

Helping children develop a support system of peers and adults is
invaluable because it provides human resources, people who can
help children cope with the stressful and painful periods in their
lives. It is also important that youngsters learn how to help others
cope in times of stress. Role-playing is a useful tool in this process.
Youngsters are given a real-life situation that requires them to
address questions similar to those listed below. Here is a hypo-
thetical situation: "It is the tenth week of school when Jennifer
transfers to your school. She misses her old friends. She feels
scared and lonely, and doesn't know anyone here at the new
school."

1. What could you do in this situation to help Jennifer feel more
   comfortable? Name as many ways as possible to assist.____
   _____
   _____

2. How can others support you?_____
   _____

3. How will you help?_____
   _____

Objectives of a Support System

You want to help youngsters

- to become aware of others' stress and how to help them;
- to understand the concept of a support system and friends.

A support system helps you in coping with problems. Your family and friends, for example, provide a support system for you. Helping others cope with their problems can make everyone's life less stressful. To help you identify your support system, write down the name of a person who provides or is a support system for you. Then see if you can determine how they support you, and ways in which they demonstrate or show that support. Here's an example:

Supporter: <u>My mom</u>

How they support me: <u>Last week when I was so scared because I had to give a book report in front of the class, my mother fixed me a special breakfast, practiced my report with me, and put a "You can do it! I love you!" note in my lunch box.</u>

What do they do to demonstrate that support? <u>She made me feel prepared. She made me feel special.</u>

A favorite pet can be a support, too. Here's how.

Supporter: <u>Kukabear</u>

How they support me: <u>Even when among friends, my puppy is loyal to me, coming and following when I call out to her.</u>

What do they do to demonstrate that support? <u>When I am sad, my puppy senses my sadness, and cuddles in my lap.</u>

Now think of two supporters of your own:

Supporter: _____
How they support me:_____
_____
_____

What do they do to demonstrate that support?_____
_____

Supporter: _____
How they support me:_____
_____

What do they do to demonstrate that support?_____
_____

Handling Emotions—Building Social Skills

It is possible to teach youngsters both to recognize other individuals' emotional responses to certain situations and to label their own feelings and emotions in similar situations. It is important for youngsters to internalize these perceptions, because they are often unaware of their own internal states as well as any external indications of emotion that others might show. They must also examine their own actions and reactions to see whether they are impulsive and whether they are getting keyed up by the other person's emotionality.

Acquiring skills for dealing with their own and other people's emotions helps youngsters develop social relationships and improves their social skills.

Once the recognition of emotions has been taught, dealing with them, whether personal or someone else's, is treated as any other problem and dealt with by generating alternatives and by consequence evaluation. The exercise below helps youngsters learn techniques for handling their peers, teachers, and parents.

1. How do you show your feelings?_____

_____

2. How do you *express* your feelings?_____

_____

3. How do you express happiness?_____

_____

4. How can you tell when other people are happy? What do they look like?_____

_____

5. What is something that makes you angry?_____

_____

6. What do people look like when they're angry?_____

_____

Certain emotions create actual feelings in our bodies. Answer the following questions:

Where do you feel happiness?_____
Where do you feel anger?_____
Where do you feel excitement?_____
Where do you feel fear?_____

Helping Others

It is sad but true that people sometimes forget to share good feelings with one another. Telling people that you have good feelings about them can be a stress reducer for them. You can share positive feelings with other people. Answer the following questions or statements:

1. Tell about something that makes you feel good._____

_____

2. Describe something you did that made someone else happy.

_____

3. Can you think of something an adult said to you this week that made you feel good? What was it?_____

_____

You can help others reduce the stress in their lives by remembering to give them positive feedback. *Feedback* is what you tell someone or by action you show someone. For example, if I notice you're wearing new shoes and I like them, I give you positive feedback by saying, "I really like your new shoes." A hug or a smile can also be positive feedback. You are sharing good feelings when you do these things.

Take a few minutes now and list three things that another person can do or say to make you feel good.

1. _____

   _____

2. _____

   _____

3. _____

   _____

After you have finished your list, share it with someone. If you have a positive feeling to give to someone special, do it now! In case you need a hint on how to get started, look at the statements below:

BEGINNING STATEMENTS

I appreciate...
I liked you when...
I missed you when...
It helped me when...
When you...I...

PARENTS: Do not assume youngsters will do or learn this on their own. Teach them how to use these statements and reinforce them when they do.

Showing Anger

Many times youngsters feel guilty about being angry—or worse yet, about expressing that anger. Being assertive means expressing feelings related to conflict as well as those of affection, gratitude, and love. Anger is a natural emotion. Typically, people react to anger in one of two ways. The first is by dumping feelings on someone—usually the result of allowing anger to build up. Sometimes this occurs long after the original incident that caused the anger, and we dump, or unload, the angry feelings on the wrong person. If this happens too frequently, it can endanger relationships. The second type of reaction to anger and/or conflict is to internalize frustration rather than express it outwardly. By not expressing these feelings, we build up resentment and pressure. The end result is often physiological or emotional symptoms of stress. An ulcer, for example, is the result of internal frustrations and turmoil. How do you show anger? Answer the following questions.

How do you express anger?_____

What do you do when you are angry?_____

Does it depend upon the person you are angry with?_____

Does it depend upon where you are at the time?_____

See if you can identify the ways you show anger. See if you can also identify those people you might get angry with.

EXAMPLE OF "WHO"	EXAMPLE OF "HOW"
1. Your best friend	A. Do nothing
2. Your brother	B. Yell
3. Your parent	C. Cry
4. Your pet	D. Slam the door
5. Your teacher	E. Walk away
6. Your sister	F. Refuse to speak to that person
7. Yourself	G. Hit him or her
8. A stranger	H. Throw something at them
9. Other	

Let's apply this skill to a real-life incident. Examine the following situations. How should the person best cope with anger?

• Chad has just discovered that his softball glove is missing from the locker. Brian informs him that he borrowed the glove last week, and then remembers that he forgot it on the practice field. The glove was a gift to Chad from his uncle and a very valued possession.
  1. What should Chad do?
  2. What should Brian do?
  3. What might happen next?
  4. How do you think Chad will react to what Brian does?
  5. How can this problem be solved to reduce Chad's anger?

• Linda and Diane are sisters. Linda has been asked by her parents to be in charge and to take care of Diane while their parents are away at work. Diane has been asked to turn off the television set and prepare for bed. Diane feels this is unfair and kicks the television's "off" button, goes to her room, and slams the door behind her.
  1. What should Linda do?
  2. What should Diane do?
  3. What might happen next?
  4. How do you think Linda will react to what Diane does?
  5. How can this problem be solved to reduce anger?
Remember, it's OK to get angry, but it is important to know you are angry and why. Even more important is to learn different ways to cope with your anger—ways that won't hurt you or anyone else and can help you solve problems.

1. Tell the person you are angry and why. Preface your statement with "I don't like it when you use my baseball

glove without first asking." This kind of statement allows the other person to know your feelings and what he did that made you angry.

2. If you are so angry that you feel as though you may actually strike someone or say something you may regret, try to cool off before expressing your feelings. Walk away, take a deep breath, think about why you are angry and what will result if you don't express it. Try to decide what to do.

3. If you are not sure what to do, or what is the right thing to do, talk to someone else about the problem. This will help you come up with the most logical solution.

4. Relax. Take a deep breath and try to relax your muscles. Talk to yourself. Reassure yourself that you want to do what is best for everyone involved.

Answer the following questions:
    How can anger cause you stress?
    What are two ways you can cope with anger?

Assertiveness

An important reason for teaching youngsters to develop assertiveness skills is so they may confidently confront situations that would typically produce anxiety, frustration, guilt, and other guilt-producing emotions. This confidence is especially important if they are to be effective in making difficult decisions. Assertiveness skills comprise a blueprint for confidence: They provide effective communications, they enable a child to be receptive to innovation, and they produce a healthy tolerance for the normal conflicts of everyday life. Basic to learning assertion skills are five types of assertion.

Simple Assertion: (Refusing a request) "No, I really don't have the time to help you now, but I'll be glad to help you with that tomorrow." (Expressing affection) "You are really very special to me."

Empathic: (Conveying recognition of other person's feeling while still communicating your own rights) "I appreciate your advice and caring, but I really need to learn to solve my own problems."

Escalating: (When a person fails to respond to minimal assertion) "No, please don't call again. I don't want you to call me at my home."

Confrontive: (When a person's actions contradict his words) "I thought we agreed I would have the opportunity to go on this trip. In the future, I would like to have your decision clarified in advance."

"I" Language: (Used for expressing negative feelings) "*I really felt upset when you didn't call.*"

There are three categories of assertion: aggressive, nonassertive, and assertive. The following example illustrates a statement in each of these categories:

The situation is that a teacher is trying to get a class back onto the topic after they've wandered into other areas.

Aggressive: "Can't you people stop goofing off and get back on the subject?"

Nonassertive: "Um... do you think we could get back on the subject (ha, ha)? I've sort of forgotten it myself."

Assertive: "I think that what we're talking about is valuable. However, I feel we need to get back to our original subject of discussion."

Practicing assertive behavior requires an understanding of these principles:

1. The child must be aware of what is going on in an interaction and of having (or taking) some control of the direction the interaction takes. This involves
   a. communicating to others what he or she thinks is going on

    b. reporting how he or she feels about what's going on in the interaction

    c. asking the other person to confirm or deny his/her goals in the situation and communicating his or her own feelings and ideas

    d. choosing not to respond or continue the interaction if it is contrary to his or her own goals

2. The child expresses honest statements.

    a. making "I" statements—that is, making statements in a direct, clear manner

    b. having the ability to be in touch with his or her needs and wants and to express them

    c. owning his or her own ideas

        1. making personal statements instead of asking questions ("I think..." instead of "Don't you think that...")

        2. shying away from quoting statements and sources when not needed

    d. describing what he or she sees objectively—not dealing in personalities or second-guessing another's motives

3. The child uses nonverbal or body language to his or her advantage.

    a. using direct and/or extended eye contact

    b. using his or her hands only when necessary for emphasis

    c. smiling only when he or she means to smile, not compulsively

    d. having good body posture: holding head erect, leaning in, facing the person he or she is talking to. The child is not tense, withdrawn, or meek and doesn't communicate with hands covering the mouth

    e. projecting his or her voice, speaking up loud and clear

    f. choosing where he or she wishes to be in a group.

The child is aware of central, visible position as opposed to sideline, protective position. The child becomes aware of the choices he or she is making.

Improving Your Self-Concept

Your self-concept is what you believe yourself to be—how you actually *feel* about yourself. Since beliefs often determine how you feel about yourself, they also influence how you act toward other people. What you think or say about yourself can and does influence your behavior. Let's see how you feel about yourself. (Both parent and child should do this exercise.)

1. List five words that best describe you.
   Parent: _____ _____ _____ _____ _____

   Child: _____ _____ _____ _____ _____
2. Now write a sentence about what you like about yourself.
   Parent: _____
   Child: _____
3. Next, in one sentence, describe what you DON'T like about yourself.
   Parent: _____
   Child: _____
4. Using the examples below as a guide, rewrite the sentence in #3 as a positive, rather than negative, statement.
   Parent: _____
   Child: _____
   Example: I hate school.
   Rewrite: I find my math class difficult, but I like the other subjects.
   Example: I'm not very popular.
   Rewrite: I'd like to be friends with Erin, but I'm not certain he wants my friendship.

If you think you are a poor student, for example, you will probably find school stressful, and this will contribute to your not liking school. Likewise, if you want someone else's friendship more than they want yours, you may feel unpopular. The messages that you send yourself are called *self-talk*. You can enhance your self-concept if you focus on the positive aspects of your abilities. When you begin to feel down, remind yourself of your good traits. Focus on the things you do well.

Think-Aloud Skills

Helping ourselves "rewrite" a feeling is a vital skill. Talking to ourselves, often called "think-aloud," is something people do a lot. But even though there are lots of times when we do talk to ourselves, there are times when we forget this process and simply *react*. Sometimes we have a problem *because* we reacted automatically, without thinking or talking to ourselves. Often this results in further difficulty that might not have existed if we had been thinking to ourselves at the time. In other words, you *can* make improvements and change and/or break the habit of responding automatically without thinking something through or stopping to consider the *consequences* (what will occur as a result of your response). Thinking *out loud* can help you through a difficult situation.

To learn how to use the think-aloud procedure, let's begin with some problems that will be easy for you. Find your way through the maze in figure 2, noting each step of the process you use to complete it.

If you precisely noted the process you used to find your way, it probably goes something like this:

> Let's see, what's my problem? I need to take my pencil and find my way from the start to the finish without crossing any lines. OK, now what's my plan? I can go slowly and look ahead. If I go down this alley, it will be a wrong turn, so I can turn around and go back. If I make a mistake and

FIG. 2
A THINK-ALOUD EXERCISE

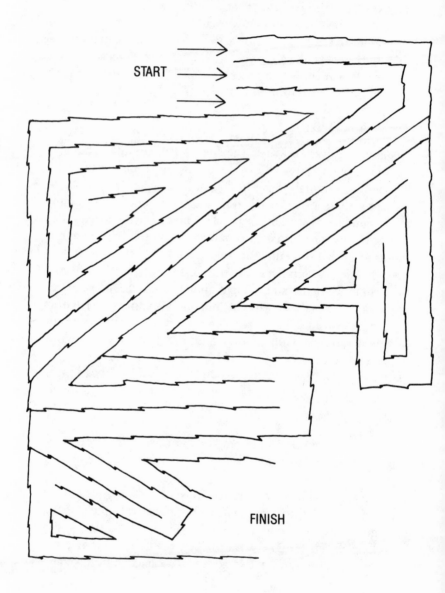

START

FINISH

cross a line, I'll just cross back again. OK, here I go. I'm going slowly and looking ahead. I'm not going down that way, because I can see it's a dead end. Whoops, I wasn't looking where I was going and I crossed a line. I'll just cross back and keep going. Am I following my plan? Most of the time. I am going slowly and looking ahead. Here I am at the finish. How did I do? Pretty well. I made a mistake, but found my way out.

Let's continue by applying the think-aloud steps to situations involving interactions with other people. Try this exercise. Look over the following dilemma. List all of the possible things (alternatives) you could do in this situation. Next, list all of the consequences of each action. Now, write down the action you have decided to apply to this dilemma.

You have made plans to attend a particular movie with your friends. Your parents have allowed you to attend because they approve of the movie. You get to the movie and it is sold out. Your friends decide to attend another movie, one that your parents have specifically forbidden you to see. It is unlikely that they will find out about this change in plans, but you know they would be greatly disappointed if they did. You want them to trust you, but you don't want to disappoint your friends, and you do want to see this movie. What will you do?

1. Verbalize THE PROBLEM_____

   _____

2. What decisions need to be made here?

   a) _____

   b) _____

   c) _____

   d) _____

3. What action will you choose?

   a) _____

   b) _____

4. What will be the likely consequences of that action?

a) _____

b) _____

How to Communicate

We depend on verbal and nonverbal communication to digest what is happening around us. Most events are neutral; they are given meaning by our perceptions, which are filtered through our expectations and knowledge. In fact, the very language we use directs our attitudes, controls our thinking processes, and modifies our behavior to a great extent. Yet we provide few first-rate experiences for youngsters in developing effective inter-personal and intrapersonal communication skills. Parents generally leave this education to chance. This is unfortunate, because poor communication skills frequently contribute to stressful relationships.

Effective communication is always a challenge and is especially difficult in today's fast-changing society. An ever-accelerated rate of change affects society as a whole and determines the kind of people we are. But even more significantly, the kind of people we are affects our communication with others, and the way we communicate affects the society in which we live. A dynamic force exists involving change, humanity, and communication. Thus, the way we interact with one another can influence others to be compassionate and can help complete our search for meaning, joy, and happiness. All of us have the need to feel capable, to feel worthwhile. Through open and shared communication, we develop our capacity for caring, for integrity, for commitment, and for responsibility. Through effective communication skills, we add to our own feelings of being worthwhile. Our goal is to help youngsters be all they can be. Such is the power of communication. Real communication focuses on caring for and fulfilling the needs of one another. Communication is a way of keeping connected in changing times.

How Are Your Communication Skills?

Communication means shared understanding and shared meaning. It is not a technique but a situation where the skills of listening, questioning, and speaking are used in a way that creates trust, a caring attitude expressed by all involved.

People often fail to communicate because they filter out much of the incoming message. Figure 3 illustrates how this barrier or filtering process affects communication.

FIG. 3
HOW MESSAGES ARE FILTERED

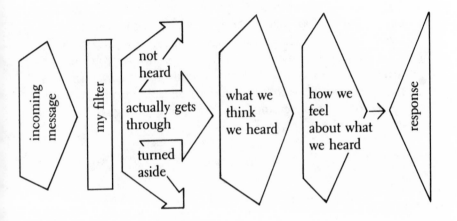

Defense Mechanisms

Youngsters' desire to protect their self-image is often much stronger than their willingness to face the truth. This leads to the use of defense mechanisms to keep that self-concept intact. Let us say, for example, that a student decides to cheat on a term paper by turning in someone else's work. The youngster might reason, "Why should I write a paper? I know lots of other students who don't, either." In this way the student makes an excuse for his or her behavior and also avoids dealing with internal conflict over cheating on the term paper.

Students, like adults, find that defense mechanisms can be most useful. The problem, of course, is that defense mechanisms hinder communication, strain relationships, and greatly contribute to internal stress. When defense mechanisms are repeatedly relied upon, they become difficult to change, and if ingrained, they become a habit. It is therefore important to help youngsters identify the defenses they employ most frequently and examine the ways in which those defenses interfere with the well-being of relationships.

We can help youngsters identify their defense mechanisms by asking them to describe situations in which they become defensive and to note the individuals—parents, peers, teachers, siblings, others—who cause them to become so. For the next week, note the times you catch yourself acting defensively. Record these observations and describe the incident in which you became defensive. See if you can identify the defense mechanism you need. Record the emotions you experienced. Finally, note the degree of stress or tension—low, medium, or high—that you experienced at the time of the incident.

DEFENSIVENESS LOG

Monday:

Tuesday:

Wednesday:

Thursday:

Friday:

Saturday:

Sunday:

1. Did you find you could identify defensiveness more quickly as the week went on?
2. Was it easier to identify defensiveness when you initiated it or when someone else did?
3. Did you notice any occasions where someone else's defensiveness was caused by a remark you made?
4. How has this exercise helped you?

Listening Skills

The technique of active listening must surely be included in any discussion concerning the importance of effective communication. Poor listening can lead to a myriad of problems in our children's interactions with others, whereas effective listening is a valuable skill for reducing stress in relationships. Active listening promotes empathy and acceptance of other people's views. The active listener demonstrates concern for and interest in the other person, and in so doing promotes a more trusting, less stressed relationship. In contrast to responding by questioning, judging, defending, or rationalizing, active listening entails feedback that is objective and nonjudgmental. The technique is particularly effective in highly emotional situations—and certainly, youngsters usually involve themselves at the emotional level. Active listening allows time for both speaker and listener to cool down and think rationally.

This concept can best be understood using the following diagram:

A <u>sends message to</u>   **B

B <u>responds to</u>   **A and says...

"You sound_____   about_____."

Some sample feedback statements:
"You really sound angry about not getting permission to go."

"You really sound upset with me because I'm late in picking you up."

"You sound really pleased with your performance on today's spelling test."

Active listening is particularly necessary when there has been a breakdown in communication, causing stress between the individuals involved. Active listening can be hard work, but it is worthwhile. By requesting adequate information and obtaining feedback, misunderstandings are minimized and defensiveness, too. Hearing a person's feelings is as important as hearing their words. Can you recall a time when you told a good friend about something and it felt good just to have him listen? Having your feelings heard is a good way to reduce stress.

If you would like to gain skills in becoming a better listener, try the following exercise.

1. Pick a partner.
2. Tell that partner about something *you* really like to do.
3. Have your partner sum up what you said, and *state* how he or she thinks you felt.
4. Do this same exercise again, only this time *you* be the (active) listener.
5. After you have completed this exercise, share your feelings.

Sometimes people don't get along simply because they misunderstand each other. This is why active listening can also be good for solving problems between people. You can use active listening to check whether you really understand another person.

Active listening means really hearing what a person is saying, and understanding how he feels. Most important, it means letting him know you heard what he said, and how he felt.

Positive (Active) Listening

It is not enough to simply *act* like a good listener. You must *be* a good listener. A good listener listens to really understand what the other person is saying. Most people do not communicate; they take turns talking. People may act like listeners but may really just be thinking of what they are going to say when it is their turn to talk.

To understand, you must

—Ask questions:
   —"How did you do that?"
   —"What did you do?"
   —"Where did you do that?"
   —"When was that?"
   —"Who did it?"
—Get more information:
   —"Tell me more about that."
—Let the talker know you are not informed on the subject:
   —"I don't know much about this."
   —"I have never been there."
   —"I have not heard of that before."
—Give feedback:
   —"Is this what you mean?" (Repeat what has been said, putting it into your own words.)
   —"Do I understand this correctly?" (Repeat as above.)

To *be* a good listener, you must *act* like a good listener.
To *act* like a good listener, you should

1. Maintain good eye contact.
2. Sit attentively. Even lean forward at times. Ask questions. Give encouragement to the talker with questions. React. Give positive feedback. This is important. People like attention and recognition. Good listening shows you *care*.

To improve your overall listening skills, try the following exercises.

A. Your ability to be a good listener is dependent on your *attitude!* You must *want* to listen to be a good listener. You tell people what you think of them by the way you listen. Discuss how your attitude toward the following would influence the way you listen to (1) someone you think beautiful and exciting; (2) someone you will never meet again; (3) someone you disagree with; (4) your very best friend.

B. One's self-concept is threatened when talking to a poor listener and improved when talking to a good listener. Explain your self-concept. How do you feel the way others listen to you affects *your* self-concept?

   It has been said that we have a greater effect on people by the way we listen than by the way we talk. How do you feel about this?

   Many times we are judged by the way we listen. How does listening affect *your* impression of another person's intelligence? Personality? Friendliness? Success? Attractiveness? Your attraction to that person?

   We tend to assume that listening is a passive activity, but positive listening requires determination and understanding. Here are some suggestions:

   1. Resist distractions. Don't try to do something else when you are listening.
   2. Don't listen only for the speaker's words; listen for his/her meaning. This will be easier if you try to put yourself in the speaker's place—try to understand his/her point of view, feelings, and intentions. Be empathic.
   3. Try not to let your feelings about the speaker or the subject affect your listening. The time to judge the worth of a statement is *after* you have heard it. Listen with an open mind.

4. Utilize feedback whenever possible to confirm or clarify the message received.

Do you have any listening habits that could be improved? Here is an inventory to help you assess your listening habits. Circle Y if you think the answer is YES, N if it's NO.

1. Do you ever turn your thoughts to other subjects when you believe a speaker will have nothing particularly interesting to say?   Y   N

2. Can you tell from a person's appearance and delivery that he/she won't have anything worthwhile to say?   Y   N

3. When you are puzzled or annoyed by what someone says, do you try to get the question straightened out immediately, either in your own mind or by interrupting the speaker?   Y   N

4. Do you listen primarily for facts rather than ideas when someone is speaking?   Y   N

5. When somebody's talking to you, do you try to make him/her think you're paying attention when you're not?   Y   N

6. When you're listening to someone, are you easily distracted by outside sights and sounds?   Y   N

7. Do you go out of your way to avoid hearing things you feel will be too difficult to understand?   Y   N

8. Do certain words, phrases, or ideas prejudice you so that you cannot listen objectively?   Y   N

9. You think about four times faster than a person usually talks. Do you use this excess time to think about other things while you're keeping general track of the conversation?   Y   N

The Benefits of Exercise

A regular exercise program provides numerous benefits, including increased strength and stamina; reduction of fatigue and incidence of disease; maintenance of ideal body weight; and strengthening of the cardiovascular and respiratory systems.

A summary of some of the benefits of exercise includes:

1. enhancement of ability to handle daily stressful encounters
2. increase in circulation
3. assistance to heart
4. additional oxygen to the body
5. benefits from the body's endorphins
6. aid to digestion
7. relaxation of nerves, balanced emotions
8. increased resistance to disease
9. reduced fatigue
10. strengthened muscles, bones, and ligaments
11. improved complexion and skin tone
12. sharpened mental powers
13. increased self-confidence

Beyond the physical effects, exercise can be a fun, social activity and can give you a general feeling of well-being and satisfaction. So urge your child to engage in some form of exercise at least three times a week. And join in yourself! It'll make it easier for your child, and it's good for you, too.

Problem-Solving Skills

Controlling Irrational Ideas

In the absence of effective coping skills, irrational ideas become a major source of stress. The nature of a child's internal dialogue, or self-talk, determines a good deal of his or her behavior and response to stressful situations. It is what a child says to himself or herself before, during, and after a stressful incident that influences feelings and behaviors. It is not so much the presence of irrational ideas that leads to disturbing emotions, but the absence of coping skills. It is important to talk to yourself during a stressful episode so you can devise reasonable solutions or reactions to the situation, and thus reduce the stress.

Sometimes, though, in times of stress, a child's self-talk is nondirected and not so productive; rather, it only adds to the level of tension. There are some situations where children aren't talking to themselves enough, but just reacting impulsively. It is the absence of coping self-talk that accounts for a child's feeling stressed in many situations. The following list illustrates three different kinds of self-talk—overreacting, underreacting, and coping—in response to a stressor.

A word of caution: It is not uncommon for some youngsters to underreact to experiences and thus deny themselves legitimate concerns. This can be better understood in the case of a child who denies any fear and actually becomes more fearful in the denial process. Underreacting can be as stressful as overreacting.

THREE TYPES OF SELF-STATEMENTS

SITUATION: Unreasonable homework assignment by a teacher.

OVERREACTING

What am I going to do? There is no way to complete this
    work!
This is really unfair!
I'm really angry.
This teacher is a real headache!
This teacher has no right to give me all this work.
Who does he think he is?
I'm going to tell this teacher exactly what I think!

UNDERREACTING

So, the teacher wants me to do this. Since I'll never get it done, I'm not going to bother at all.
I can handle all this, but I'll wait until I'm in the mood to do it.

COPING

What's going on here?
That individual expects me to do all this?
That's a little upsetting, but what is it I need to do?
Worrying won't help. Just think for a minute, organize.
Should I talk it over with the teacher and ask for more time?
OK, I can handle it, if I just relax, go slowly, get a plan, get organized, and begin.
I'll ask for help whenever I need it. Good, I think I can handle the situation now.
And if I can't finish it all, I'll know I've done my best. The teacher will see that and probably won't be angry at me.

Alternative or desired feelings and behavior result from cognitive self-analysis. Most of us would prefer feeling mildly irritated to feeling very angry or upset.

It is important to provide youngsters with a systematic approach to achieving a greater awareness of their own faulty thinking patterns that lead to stress. Asking youngsters to identify stressful situations, analyze, generate rational alternatives, and project how they would like to feel in the situation helps them develop cognitive self-analysis skills. The following work sheet will be helpful with youngsters.

COGNITIVE SELF-ANALYSIS

A. EVENT (as you initially perceive it)	B. THOUGHTS ABOUT "A"
C. FEELINGS AND BEHAVIORS	D. EVENT (as you think about it later)
E. ALTERNATIVE THOUGHTS	F. FEELINGS AND BEHAVIORS (desired)

Developing Alternatives

Much of the stress that youngsters encounter stems from their inability to generate a broad range of alternatives in their attempt to solve problems effectively. Youngsters who cannot cope with reality opt to cop out.

Effective problem-solving is learned by confronting events, defining problems, experimenting, searching for sound solutions. Successful problem-solving requires that the child summon all of his or her resources to generate alternatives and find solutions. It is a creative process. *It is also a learned skill.* Problem-solving is best learned by confronting real problems. Many of us have been more preoccupied with helping our children acquire academic knowledge than in teaching effective problem-solving skills. Children need to learn the skills of problem-solving in order to reduce stress, maintain stability, and achieve worthwhile goals. And as an adult, being an effective problem-solver will lead to success in all areas of life, both personal and professional.

There are a number of ways to help youngsters learn the process of problem-solving. One very effective approach is the *think-aloud technique* discussed on p. 145.

Going through the following work sheet will help your youngster develop a more organized approach to problem-solving.

PROBLEM-SOLVING

I. **WHAT IS THE PROBLEM?**
Situation:

> Peter called me an idiot and it made me mad!

Present method of coping or reacting:
a.

II. **HOW CAN I SOLVE IT?**
Alternatives to present methods (list all possibilities)

Plan for coping (choose from above):
a.
b.
c.
Goals:

> 1. I could call him an idiot back.
> 2. I could punch him out.
> 3. I could tell him how angry it makes me.
> 4. I could ignore it.

III. **WHAT IS MY PLAN?**
(Choose one of the alternatives listed above)

Revised Plan, if necessary. (Any parts that aren't working?)

> 1. I'm going to tell him to stop name-calling.

IV. **HOW DID I DO?**
Goals met: (If not, what is another plan I could try?)

> Great. I said it politely and then I didn't get in a fight this time. Maybe he'll stop.

Goals not met:

Here is another example of this process:

1. *What's my problem?* It's almost time for school and I haven't completed my homework yet.
2. *How can I solve it?* I could ask my mother for help. I could get busy and do it now. I could tell my teacher I need more time.
3. *What's my plan?* I'll get busy now. I don't think I'll leave it to the morning again!
4. *How did I do?* OK. It's not as neat as I would like, but it is completed, and I believe it's done fairly well.

Some problems are very difficult to understand. Thinking of creative ways to solve difficult problems is called "devising alternatives."

Here is more practice. Try solving these dilemmas.

1. Dean has baseball practice on Saturday at 2:00. His very best friend is having a birthday party at that same time.
   What is Dean's problem?_____

   _____

   _____
   What are Dean's alternatives?_____

   _____

   _____

2. Amy is supposed to take her report card home to her parents today. Amy is afraid because she has two low grades. She also wants to invite a friend to stay overnight for the evening, but is afraid her parents will say no because of her low grades. She would like to show her parents the report card tomorrow!
   What is Amy's problem?_____

What are Amy's alternatives?_____

_____

_____

When you decide on a certain alternative, you need to remember that each alternative has a *consequence*. A consequence is something that happens when a particular alternative is chosen—for example, what might happen if Amy decided to give the report to her parents today?

What are the possible consequences of the alternatives you chose for Dean's problem?_____

_____

What are the possible consequences of the alternatives you chose for Amy's problem?_____

_____

Helping youngsters identify a situation that is causing stress in their life, then outlining the problem and defining the specific behavior the youngster wants to change, teaches children to formulate plans that deal with problems.

More About Consequences

The preceding work sheet asked youngsters to consider the consequences of various alternatives they are considering in solving a problem. You can help your youngster examine the likely outcome of proposed actions by asking questions like "If you did that, what do you think would happen?" or "Would you want that to happen to you?" These questions are often followed by "And then what would happen?" If the youngster proposes solutions that are not very realistic, guide him/her back to reality by asking, "What is the problem?" or "What is the plan?"

Most children cannot easily supply a "plan," which is basically solving a specific problem, and need direction on how to do this. Continually encourage the youngster to elaborate more alternatives to the problem and then to realistically assess the potential impact of each of these options.

The overall goal is to help youngsters (1) define the real problem, (2) generate alternative solutions for that problem, (3) evaluate what the effects and consequences of those solutions would be, and (4) decide on a plan of action. This plan of action can then be practiced by role-playing. The goal here is to help youngsters learn that there is more than one way of handling a problem, that not all solutions work equally well, and that thinking before you act can lead to a better outcome.

THINKING ABOUT CONSEQUENCES

When we think of a way to solve a problem, we call this an "alternative." When we decide on a certain alternative, we need to remember that each alternative has a *consequence*. A consequence is something that happens when a particular alternative is chosen. Try this exercise:

Peter has just received a call from Brian, who wants Jennifer to come over to his house to play. But since Peter and Jennifer are playing now, Peter doesn't want to tell Jennifer that Brian has called, so he doesn't.

1. What is the problem here?_____

_____

2. What are some of Peter's alternatives?_____

_____

3. What are the possible consequences of Peter's dilemma?____

_____

4. What are the possible consequences of the alternatives you chose for Peter's dilemma?_____

_____

Tender Loving Care

Another important factor in preventing stress is receiving an abundance of tender loving care (commonly known as TLC) from significant others. Recently, its value was demonstrated accidentally in a research project studying cholesterol deposits in rabbits. Although all were fed the same diet, it was discovered that some of the rabbits had markedly reduced cholesterol deposits. Initially the researchers couldn't explain why this had happened. Then they discovered that a night lab worker had been playing with some of the rabbits, giving certain rabbits his attention and affection as he was cleaning the lab. These rabbits developed fewer cholesterol deposits.

Once they learned this, the researchers repeated the study, this time deliberately giving certain rabbits more attention, fondling, and affection. Again the rabbits that received the tender loving care had fewer cholesterol deposits. Numerous other studies show the powerful effects of "TLC" and its potential for contributing to overall wellness for humans.

What do you do when you recognize that you need more "stroking" from the significant people in your life? Do you wait for demonstrations of affection, or have you learned appropriate ways to get your needs fulfilled?

> Complete this exercise:
> When I need affection from others, I_____.
> I need affection most when_____.

Metacognition

An important point in teaching children self-control is the function of what is termed "metacognition"—"knowing about knowing," "thinking about thinking." It is what people say to themselves before, during, and after performing a task. Our focus here is on helping youngsters become aware of their "metacognitions" so they can control their behavior by thinking about thinking.

The only direct way to alter the influence of our own thoughts (including images, self-instructions, and feelings) is to become aware of these thoughts and actively alter them. One way to do this is to concentrate on (imagine or guess) the probable outcome of an action, and thereby alter the action. Another is to alter the thoughts directly, "I'm going to hit him" would be altered to "I really feel like hitting him, but if I do, I'll be punished. I'd better think of a better way to handle this." "I'm really depressed" becomes "I feel depressed, but look at all the good things I've accomplished today. Hey, I must be a pretty good person after all."

Teaching Youngsters How to Develop Inner Speech

There are three basic stages by which the initiation and inhibition of behavior come under verbal control. The first stage focuses on the speech of others. Here adults control and direct the child's behavior. The second is characterized by the child's ability to regulate his or her behavior, and the third stage by the child's ability to assume a self-governing role for behavior.

In teaching youngsters to talk to themselves as a means of developing self-control, a five-step process has been developed, which can be applied to various situations.

1. An adult performs the task while talking to himself out loud.
2. The child performs the same task under the direction of the adult.
3. The child performs the task while instructing himself aloud.
4. The child whispers the instructions to himself as he goes through the task.
5. The child performs the task while guiding his performance via inaudible or private speech or nonverbal self-direction.

In using this approach, the parent must demonstrate and monitor the important skills listed below:

1. Defining the problem. ("Let's see now, I must get these three errands done before noon.")
2. Facilitating appropriate responses. ("How much time will I need?" or "I'll need about an hour and a half.")
3. Self-reinforcement. ("Great. So far, so good.")
4. Corrected errors. ("I forgot my shopping list at home. Well, OK. I'll need a few more minutes to go back and get it.")

The parent supplies a portion of the self-instruction for the youngster, being careful not to supply all of it. Similarly, it is important that solutions be generated by the youngster. If the solution has been created by the child, he or she is more likely to "own" the solution and thus demonstrate commitment to using it.

Periodically, children need to block inappropriate internal dialogue, and for this they will need special skills and strategies. They must learn how to say to themselves, "Stop," in order to break into the thought processes, and then say, "Take it easy. I think I can solve the problem."

The overall lesson is to give youngsters a method for interrupting high-probability misbehavior such as acting out hostility. In such a situation, the child is taught to interrupt his ongoing thoughts, which are likely to be focused on his anger, and instead to experience the problem through role-playing, discussing, or visualizing the situation, and to then stop and think, "Wait a minute. Relax and take a breath. How is this going to help me? Is there some other solution?"

Again, the goal is to have the youngster alter his ongoing thought processes by saying "Stop" to himself, relaxing a bit, and then thinking before he takes some action that may be irrevocable. This process helps the youngster to anticipate the full impact of his actions based upon acceptable rules, to avoid negative consequences as much as possible, and to gain control of himself and his behavior.

Here is an example to use with youngsters:

Exercise

Think of a time when you had several things to do, but little time to do them. Were you aware of using "inner speech"? Here's an example: You have just arrived at school. In a few minutes the bell will ring. Your internal dialogue probably will go something like this: "Let's see now. Before I get to class, I need to stop at my locker and get my book. Then I need to go by the office and turn in my permission-to-be-off-campus slip, and on the way back I need to stop and buy pencils at the bookstore. First I'll go to my locker. There's Jim—no, I must not stop to chat, because I'll be late." Or: "I've got my book. Now, to the office. Let me just find the permission slip my father wrote this morning. . . ."

This example typifies the use of internal language. By using this, we are able to control our behavior.

When we are learning a new skill or encounter a new situation, inner speech becomes much more prominent, sometimes even becoming spoken out loud. But as we master the new skill, the out-loud speech tends to disappear, and behavior becomes automatic.

Managing Time

Time is the one resource that is distributed equally to each of us. We all have 168 hours a week, 24 hours a day, 60 minutes an hour, 60 seconds a minute. Although we figuratively speak of saving, spending, or wasting time, no one has been able to create or retrieve time, accumulate or suspend time, accelerate or delay time.

A frequent stressor is the need to juggle time—attempting to cram several activities into an unrealistic time span. Students often have difficulty managing their time, and time pressures can mean distress. In youngsters this distress is often evidenced through skin disorders; headaches; inability to establish regular sleeping habits; hostility; aggression; and even violence.

Here are some helpful guidelines:

1. Be *pro*active, not reactive. Learn to anticipate and plan for stress.
2. Plan your time. Try not to be controlled by events and persons around you beyond your own personal limits. Assert yourself so that others do not push you beyond these limits. Communicate to others and to yourself what your limits are. Become aware of the signals of hyperstress.
3. Identify and plan for quality time. This is a time during the day where you can focus your awareness on a specific task without interruption. Avoid doing more than one thing at a time.
4. Become aware of your own rhythms. There are certain times during the day and month that you function better than at other times. Accept this rhythm in yourself and use this personal characteristic to your advantage by planning for it rather than to your disadvantage by fighting it.
5. Don't place demands on yourself that you can't meet. Be honest with yourself and others. Demanding too much of yourself causes stress and may create failure.
6. Know where your time goes. If necessary, make a list of what you did during a day and evaluate whether you spent your time wisely.
7. Build on your strengths—not your weaknesses. Concentrate on what you can do rather than what you cannot do.
8. Be aware that, in general, *poor* time management includes:
   a. Excess time spent in crisis situations.
   b. More time spent on trivia than is necessary.
   c. Frequent interruptions that destroy planning incentive and momentum.

    d. Less time spent on high-priority items than low-priority ones.

    e. Little quality time spent on items requiring creativity and productivity.

  9. It is necessary to set long-term life career goals as well as short-term goals.

 10. Reward yourself for what you do well. Put what you don't do well in the proper perspective.

To assist yourself in begining a time management program, use the activity-prioritizing form below to plan your days. List the tasks you must complete according to their proper importance. Allow for unforeseen additions that will come up during the day. After a while you will be able to complete this process mentally. But go over this list at the end of the day and see if you evaluated the tasks correctly. Constant reevaluation creates awareness. Awareness reduces stress.

Learn how to:

—*Budget Time.* One of the greatest pressures on a youngster is time. There seems never to be enough of it. But learning to budget time is both possible and essential.

—*Daily "To Do Lists."* A very important step in learning to manage time is to set up a daily "To Do List." Everyone should have a daily "To Do List." It does not need to be long and detailed, but should contain ten or fifteen things to be accomplished each day. Priority-setting is important. Write down your four to six tasks to be completed, then prioritize them. Set a timetable and estimate the length of time necessary to perform each task. Start with number one. You can do only one thing at a time. This way, you will take care of the more important items. Set deadlines for each item. Delegate as many of the items on your list as possible.

Prioritize your daily or weekly activities below. List them in order from most important to least important. Make a note of the approximate time each will take.

TASKS	TIME	WHO WILL I ASK FOR HELP IF NEEDED
1.		
2.		
3.		
4.		
5.		
6.		

CONCLUDING WORDS

Stress doesn't have to be a damaging condition for youngsters. With some hard work, with appropriate use of the skills and exercises provided here, and with love, we can help our children meet the challenge of growing up morally sound, physically healthy, and personally competent in our ever more dangerous and difficult world.